Fresh-Brewed Life

Fresh-Brewed Life

A Stirring Invitation to Wake Up Your Soul

NICOLE JOHNSON

THOMAS NELSON
Since 1798

NASHVILLE   DALLAS   MEXICO CITY   RIO DE JANEIRO

Published in Nashville, Tennessee, by Thomas Nelson. Thomas Nelson is a trademark of Thomas Nelson, Inc.

Thomas Nelson, Inc., titles may be purchased in bulk for educational, business, fund-raising, or sales promotional use. For information, please e-mail SpecialMarkets@ThomasNelson.com.

Unless otherwise indicated, Scripture quotations are taken from the HOLY BIBLE: NEW INTERNATIONAL VERSION®. © 1973, 1978, 1984 by International Bible Society. Used by permission of Zondervan Publishing House. All rights reserved.

Scripture quotations marked ESV are taken from the ENGLISH STANDARD VERSION. © 2001 by Crossway Bibles, a division of Good News Publishers.

An exhaustive search was done to determine whether previously published material included in this book required permission to reprint. If there has been an error, a correction will be made in subsequent editions.

"A Story to Live By" by Ann Wells, © 1997, *Los Angeles Times*. Reprinted by permission.

Library of Congress Cataloging-in-Publication Data

Johnson, Nicole, 1966–
  Fresh brewed life : a stirring invitation to wake up your soul / Nicole Johnson.
    p. cm.
  Includes bibliographical references.
  ISBN 978-1-4002-0315-4 (alk. paper)
  1. Christian women—Religious life. 2. Christian women—Conduct of life. I. Title.
BV4527.J637 2011
248.8'43—dc22   2011002745

Printed in the United States of America

11 12 13 14 15 16 QG 6 5 4 3 2 1

With fond memories of the classic story
"Rip Van Winkle," which demonstrated that
it's never too late to wake up

Contents

Contents

Introduction

Taking Your First Sip

Awake, my soul!
—PSALM 57:8

I have come that they may have life,
and have it to the full.
—JOHN 10:10

Would you like coffee this morning?

There is rarely a morning out when this offer fails to bring joy to my heart. At home the first thing I do in the morning is put on the coffee. Just the sound of the brewing perks me up. Often my soul does a little dance when the aroma of freshly ground beans starts to fill the kitchen.

Coffee brings warmth and comfort to my life. Part ritual, part relationship, part hope, having a cup in my hand feels as natural as holding a pencil. It stirs up memories and gratitude inside me.

My grandmother Audrey introduced me to coffee. She would make me coffee-milk in the morning before anyone else got up. I must have been four or five, holding my current favorite stuffed companion and still sucking my thumb. I would pad, sleepy-eyed, into the kitchen, where the kettle was simmering. The only light in the room was the one on the stove, and my grandmother would be sitting on a stool next to the counter, sipping coffee. She would glide across the floor in green nylon slippers and fix me a little cup of coffee-milk. Sweet and warm beyond compare. Sharing a little cup became our secret ritual. I thought it was my reward for waking up early. She would pull a chair close for me, and we would talk for a bit. I felt very grown-up.

Years later would find me in junior high, sitting around a huge table in Alabama with my dad's family, observing the coffee ritual, but not participating yet. I wasn't old enough. My father's brothers and sisters need nothing more than a coffeepot for celebration. Okay, one of Grandma's caramel cakes helped a bit, but they would sit for hours with coffee and with one another. I would take it all in, learning what "coffee" meant to them: love, sharing, and connection.

May you live all the days of your life.

—Jonathan Swift

Coffee is an invitation. When someone invites you to get coffee, it isn't because he or she is thirsty; more likely, that person just wants to spend time with you. Coffee calls us out of hiding. In the midst of our busy lives, we still manage time for coffee. When someone puts on a pot of coffee, people come from everywhere. It draws us out of our usual hangouts into the center of activity.

Coffee is also a universal welcome. It is readily available to all of us, rich or poor. Whichever country we live in or visit, whatever language we speak—we can always find a cup of coffee. I'm figuring I've had coffee in forty-eight of the fifty states and in at least fifteen different countries. The message is always the same: *Here is a cup of friendship and warmth; you are welcome here.*

People who don't even like coffee usually enjoy the smell and/or experience of it. I have friends who don't drink coffee but never pass up an opportunity to "get coffee" together. Although they order hot chocolate or a smoothie or some other beverage, they want to embrace the invitation to get together and sit for a while.

Coffee also offers a wake-up call. The coffee bean contains caffeine, a mild stimulant found naturally in the berries—and also found in tea and cocoa beans. In small to moderate amounts, caffeine can promote wakefulness and has been shown to increase brain activity (for short periods, not for life, unfortunately). Coffee can also produce feelings of well-being and greater awareness of one's surroundings. This makes sense to me, as I find I pay much closer attention when my eyes are open.

However I confess, in college, with too many papers and not enough evening, coffee played a different role. I sought to prove that more of a good thing would be better. It wasn't. In fact, this bad experiment cured me of "using" coffee as a stimulant because it had such an awful effect on my central nervous system. Once I had heart palpitations and anxiety that lasted almost twenty-four hours. So rest assured, I'm not seeking to create coffee addicts. Besides, to take pleasure in coffee and benefit from all it has to offer, it must be savored, not merely consumed.

But my favorite characteristic of coffee is the deep metaphor it holds for life. The process of making a cup of fresh-brewed coffee has given me words and insight as to what has made a fresh-brewed life for me, and what can make a fresh-brewed

> **Life is either a daring adventure or nothing.**
>
> —Helen Keller

life for anyone. The coffee part is fairly simple: a whole coffee bean goes into the fire, emerges richer and darker, is ground up into tiny pieces, and when hot water pours over those grinds, a magical aroma and flavor are released, and a remarkable drink is created.

Because the life part is not quite as simple as the coffee part, we'll spend the rest of the book exploring how our lives can become fresh brewed. You're invited to begin stirring your soul to wake up the slumbering parts and throw out the two-day-old, stale stuff in the bottom of the glass carafe. This is not freeze-dried life, like the Sanka your grandmother drank. We're after the real McCoy—authentic, energizing, stimulating, robust life.

Fresh-Brewed Life is a journey of awakenings:

- to God, as we learn to respond to his compelling love for us
- to ourselves, as we recognize our true identity and it illuminates us from the inside out
- to others, as we relate in new and healthy ways that bring joy and peace

Coffee is far more than a beverage. The dark substance in the cup transcends water poured over ground-up beans. It is an invitation to life. Yours.

We only live once, and if we do it well, once is enough. This book holds ten cups of fresh-brewed life. Remember, with coffee we have to sit awhile, so don't rush; just take it one cup at a time. See if you find the Creator of all coffee finding you and drawing you out of hiding, welcoming you, issuing the same invitation: *Wake up to a richer, fuller, more flavorful life than you ever imagined.*

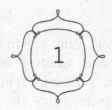

Surrender to God

You reach for the brass door handle and pull. As the seal of the door is broken, the vacuum-packed freshness envelops your senses. You step inside to warmth that wraps around your soul like a cashmere scarf. Your whole person is enveloped by the aroma. The familiar sound of hissing steam works on your stress level like a pressure release valve. You've entered a special coffee shop, and you're helpless. You give yourself over. Surrender.

You're staying in the home of a good friend. You have no responsibilities this morning, so you leisurely wake up on your own. You blink to focus and take in the room. Your clothes are lying across the chair. The sunlight is streaming in through the window, playing on the corner of the bedspread. Then from down the stairs and around the corner, the invitation finds you. Your nose has discovered the promise of a good start to the day still ahead, fresh-brewed coffee. It draws you out from under the covers. You pull on clothes as you make your way toward the promise. Surrender.

She's sitting in *her* chair. She's been awake for hours. From the time you were little, you remember her being up before everyone else. Bible open, coffee cup in her hands, beginnings of breakfast on the counter awaiting her return. Peaceful and calm. Still. The warmth of her spirit is met with the warmth of his love. A sacred, rewarding ritual. Her heavenly Father and a cup of coffee. She knows him, and he knows her. Surrender.

The fresh-brewed life is a spiritual journey from beginning to end. It is a call to wake up that begins in a relationship with the One in whom we began. God alone can tell us what we most want to know. He alone is the Rock strong enough to anchor our lives in the midst of the storms we encounter. And as we journey, it is God and only God who can go deep enough to rouse our sleepy souls.

I could not rouse my sleepy soul alone. I could not keep the pilot light of faith lit consistently enough to make the kind of difference I longed for. I've tried getting up at four thirty in the morning to have a quiet time with the Lord. Trust me: it was quiet. I have fallen asleep on God on more occasions than I would like to count. I have tried to memorize chapters of Scripture only to conclude that I must have killed off so many brain cells with artificial sweeteners, trying to be thin, that I'll never be able to be holy. Somehow I mistakenly thought that Jesus said, "Come unto me, all you who are weary and heavy laden, and I will give you more to do than anyone else!" My constant struggle to be "godly" left me tired, empty, lonely, and questioning.

I was either going to have to take pretending to a whole new level or choose to stop pretending altogether, and I wasn't sure which I would be able to pull off. I deeply identified with the story "The Emperor's New Clothes," and many days I felt like the king, pretending I "saw" the invisible clothes when there were no clothes. I was afraid to let go of my pretense, to simply confess I didn't see in my faith what other people seemed to see in theirs. In the Hans Christian Andersen story, everyone knew the emperor was naked, but they held on to pretending because they were afraid to tell the truth. They didn't trust themselves amid all the others who said they "saw," so they repeated the lie. It took an honest little boy to wake everyone up. Unfortunately for the king, the timing couldn't have been worse.

This was true for Joan as well, who spent all of the first day of her vacation sunbathing on the roof of her hotel. She wore a bathing suit that first day, but on the second she decided that, since no one could see her in her little roof spot, she would slip out of it to get an overall tan.

She'd hardly begun soaking up the rays when she heard someone running up the metal stairs and opening the door to the rooftop. Joan had been lying on her stomach, so quickly she pulled another towel over her backside to cover up.

"Excuse me, miss," said the flustered assistant manager, out of breath from running up the stairs. "The hotel doesn't mind your sunbathing on the roof, but we'd appreciate your wearing a swimsuit as you did yesterday."

"What difference does it make?" Joan asked calmly. "No one can see me up here, and besides, I'm covered with a towel."

"Not exactly," said the embarrassed gentleman. "You're lying on the dining room skylight."

Talk about exposed! It's terrifying until you realize one thing: when you're naked and everyone knows it, you've got nothing to hide anymore. For Joan or the emperor or me, the higher the level of pretending, the farther there is to fall. But once you've fallen, once you've realized how naked you really are, you're free to start living differently. There is a reason Jesus said the truth would set us free. Until we are honest, we can't have an honest relationship with him, or anyone, for that matter.

I felt a gentle stirring in my soul, like a whisper prompting me to lay it all down. "Jesus came to give you life." *Life? What is life if it isn't running all the time?* Peace—real peace on the inside, from all this climbing, striving, and worrying. Joy—unabashed delight in life, regardless of the circumstances. Love—foundational, unconditional, never-ending love. I didn't have to work for these; I had to surrender to them. More simply, I had to stop long enough to let them overtake me.

I let it go. I surrendered. I gave up being in charge of my spiritual goodness, because I could freely admit I didn't really have much spiritual goodness. I had worked for God for years and yet withheld my full heart from him. I'd sought to please him, treating him like a father who is hard to please, missing, or ignoring that he was pleased with me. I tried to do so many things *for* God that I missed being *with* God. Where was the goodness in that? I was the keeper of the covenant. I was the one making the sacrifice. I thought what Jesus did for me would be repaid by what I was doing for him! God must have grown weary watching me and my spiritual calisthenics. If we just roll up our sleeves and try harder, we are not walking with Jesus at all. If we can do it all ourselves, why do we need God?

This first cup of fresh-brewed life is crucial. A bigger spiritual "to do" list or a calendar full of church activities will not change our lives. When we give ourselves to God—mind, body, soul, and spirit—*he* changes us. We cannot change ourselves. We don't have enough spiritual stamina to change an entrenched habit, let alone our hearts. But when the walls come down and God is given access to the deepest parts of who we are, His love courses through us in a cleansing, holy, life-changing way. Our souls become stronger,

What is my only comfort in life and death? That I belong body and soul to my faithful savior Jesus Christ.
—Heidelberg Catechism

deeper, and more robust. As different as instant coffee is from fresh-brewed, we are transformed.

Discovering in Christ the Whole-Bean Essence of Who We Are

After putting her children to bed, a mother changed into sweats and a droopy T-shirt, took off her makeup, and proceeded to wash her hair. As she heard the children getting more and more rambunctious, her patience grew thin.

At last she threw a towel around her head and stormed into their room, putting them back to bed with stern warnings. As she left the room, she heard her three-year-old say with a trembling voice, "Who was that?"

> **Faith is not making religious sounding noises in the day time. It is asking your inmost self questions at night— and getting up and going to work.**
>
> —Mary Jean Irion

Have you ever lain awake at night, wondering similarly, *Who am I*? Have you ever felt as though you were faking your life? That you were living someone else's life, and you're not sure whose? Maybe there had been some terrible mix-up and you picked up another person's life by mistake? Maybe you want to give yourself to God, but what self are you going to give?

The work life that doesn't even come close to fully representing who you are? What you look like on the outside, or how you appear to others? Your relationships? Although you may feel differently, your roles as wife, mother, and friend are not the sum total of your identity. So what do we surrender to God? Or more accurately, whom do we surrender?

The answer is: all of the above.

The simile that seems to fit best about our "personhood" is

that we are like onions. We can't merely peel away all the layers, because the layers are us too. You don't get to the middle of an onion to find an apple core. The onion begins at the core, and each and every layer builds upon the "onion-ness" inside. An authentic life comes from an authentic self in which the layers on the outside are merely expressions of the core on the inside. So all the roles we play tell us something, but they are not the deepest level of our identity.

So all of it is what we surrender to God. We bring all that we know of ourselves to all that we know of God, and we enter a relationship like none other. Even when we can't figure out if all the pieces even add up to a whole person, we bring them and offer them. Then, in the loving way only God can, he begins to help us make sense of the pieces.

What you do doesn't determine who you are in the core of your being, but it does reflect what you believe (rightly or wrongly) is at the core of your being. People rarely act inconsistently with who they see themselves to be.

Remember Hans Christian Andersen's story "The Ugly Duckling"? The poor little creature was born into the barnyard and never found his place. Among the ducks, he was bitten and made fun of for being so ugly. The duckling tried everything to be a better duck—he just wanted to fit in with the other animals. Nothing he did worked, no matter how hard he tried. He was utterly miserable and ran away from the barnyard.

Rejected and having suffered through the winter alone, he ventured out in the spring to a beautiful lake nearby. He was swimming on the water when the most amazing thing happened. The ugly little ducking saw a new reflection. He wasn't a duck at all; he was a swan. A beautiful, graceful swan.

If only he had known that swans make terrible ducks, and even worse chickens, and still worse, cats—all of which the duckling had tried to be. It wasn't until he recognized who he was and what he was, that the externals began to made sense. His inner identity changed his outer behavior. And more, it moved him from trying to prove his worth to accepting his given value.

The world and even the church is quite a bit like the "barnyard." It is more than happy to define our worth based on all the externals. There are plenty of "experts" around who feel more than confident telling us where we "fit" and who we must be in order to meet certain expectations. But only God can reveal the truth to us. Because only God knows the truth about our deepest identity. In *Clinging*, Emilie Griffin explains it like this, "He will whisper it to us not in the mad rush and fever of our striving and our fierce determination to be someone, but rather when we are content to rest in Him, to put ourselves into His keeping, into His hands."

Surrendering to God the whole-bean essence of who we are will allow him access to the deepest place of our heart. The place where we hold all the messages we've heard and believed about who we really are. It is only there that God can bring about the deep change that we long for—because until we know the truth in that inner place, we will wander around noisy barnyards, seeking to make our way instead of gliding across the water in the grace of his love and acceptance.

And the day came when the risk [it took] to remain tight in the bud was more painful than the risk it took to blossom.

—Anaïs Nin

Several years ago, God used a little book called *Life of the Beloved* by Henri Nouwen to whisper this truth to me: "'You are the Beloved,' and all I hope is that you can hear these words as spoken to you with all the tenderness and force that love can hold. My only desire is to make these words reverberate in every corner of your being—'You are the Beloved.'" I looked down into the pool and saw it for the first time. Not the me that I always saw in the mirrors of the world, but the me that God saw when he created me. A baby, a girl, a youth, a woman deeply loved and valued as a daughter of a King.

This is our deepest identity. We are loved passionately by God.

Now, having written this, I have to tell you, I don't really know *why* the Creator of the universe allowed his heart to be captured in such a way by his own creation. I can't fully fathom how he can love us in such a powerful and personal way. It is a mystery, and it must remain a mystery. To understand it could make it possible to dismiss it as we are prone to dismiss other loves in our lives. If we discovered that God loved us because we were smart, who wouldn't try to be smarter so God would love us more? When we met someone much smarter than ourselves, we would have to acknowledge that God loved that person more. I suppose it's why we will never know the reason he loves us as passionately as he does. Perhaps there isn't a reason—it just is.

> It is our light, not our darkness, that most frightens us. We ask ourselves, "Who am I to be brilliant, gorgeous, talented and famous?" Actually, who are you not to be? You are a child of God.
>
> —Nelson Mandela

Why do we love our children? We can't fully explain it; we just do. Understanding why is less important to me than simply knowing that he does. So I surrender to it. I take him at his word. I just collapse on it and rest in it.

I rest because he has said nothing would take his love from me, or you. I can't say that would be true of any other human kind of love. In fact, it's so different from "regular" love that it's hard to believe that it could be really true. So God pursues us, courts us, and woos us to remind us. As if he wants to keep us mindful that he doesn't get tired of us, he isn't frustrated by our moods or by our irritating habits or put off by uncombed hair or out-of-style clothes. We are free to place the whole weight of our needs on him, to bring him our deepest questions, to look to him for acceptance and validation. And unlike any other relationship, the God who designed us will not lean, crumble, struggle, stagger, or falter in any way.

This is a love that changes everything.

Surrendering to Be Finely Ground

If it's true that the darker the roast of the coffee, the more intense the flavor, then it stands to reason that for a rich, strong life, we are going to have to go through the fire. We are also going to have to trust that this "roasting" can and will deepen our walk. The finer the grind of the beans, the more concentrated the coffee. And who among us hasn't had to endure the daily grind and still even more difficult trials? Trials have come, the Scripture says, "so that your faith—of greater worth than gold, which perishes even though refined by fire—may be proved genuine" (1 Peter 1:7). Our faith becomes genuine as we struggle. The easy faith of the "church of happy circumstances" is replaced by fire-roasted, holding-on-to-him-for-dear-life faith. And this faith is worth more than gold.

Many years ago, I was in Phoenix on a business trip. I was listening to my voice mails about work and jotting down the pertinent numbers. I wasn't prepared to hear my sister's voice, and even less prepared for her message, "Dad's had a heart attack, and he's in the hospital . . ." I knew she was trying not to frighten me. "He's in stable condition, but they're running tests." My heart was racing. I was thinking how I could cancel what I had scheduled on this trip in order to get to Alabama. "Everything is under control, and there is really nothing you could do here, so don't worry, but please pray." My sister knew me. While I appreciated her control and reassurances, I had to get there.

I canceled my appointments, booked a flight, and got on the plane. When I sat down in 23B, I started to cry. *What if something happens to him and I don't make it there in time? When was the last time I told him I loved him?* I sat in my seat, weeping. The flight attendant kindly brought me tissues. I told her I was flying home to be with my dad, who had suffered a heart attack. She told me she had just lost her dad two years ago, and then we cried together. She was so sweet to me, and I felt such sadness for her loss in that moment, and while our conversation did not make me feel better, it did open my eyes and heart in a new way. When we are in pain, we look for others who are in pain. I wondered how many others on this plane had loved ones who were ill. I wondered why I'd never had a thought like this before. I'd never gotten on a plane, looking for someone who might be hurting. I kinda shuddered to think how many people I'd probably passed in airports or on planes, never even noticing their tears or pain. Suffering has a way of opening our eyes. C. S. Lewis has been quoted as saying God "shouts in our pains. It is his megaphone to rouse a deaf world."

It saddens me that many of us need to have pain as a wake-up call. Now I try my best not to stand on the sidelines of life with deadened, dulled, disinterested senses until another shock makes me suddenly aware of the magic, marvel, and mystery of it all.

—Sarah Ban Breathnach

I made it to Nashville and drove five hours to the hospital. Despite the length of the trip and how much I'd thought about

Dad along the way, nothing could have prepared me to see my strong, military father lying in a hospital bed, pale and still with an oxygen tube in his nose and an IV in his arm. I thought I had cried all my tears before I got there, but I was wrong. I thought I had flown all that way just to hold him, but in that moment, I really needed him to hold me. I was so very afraid. And hold me he did. His embrace alone told me he would be all right.

Jesus himself had to surrender to God. When he prayed, "Not my will, but thine be done," he was demonstrating his willingness to lay down his own agenda. It's possible this is the most terrifying prayer in all of Scripture. It's the ultimate picture of trust—*I have a will, but rather than use it for my own agenda, I'm going to trust that from what I know of you, it is your will that I want. Even if it will break my heart, we'll go with your plan.*

How can we get to this kind of surrender but through prayer? Just as Jesus did, we bring our lives (and our wills) to him, wrestling all the way, and offer to trust his way rather than our own. Notice I didn't write, "Just bring your problems to Jesus and get over them." Not only do I not believe that our problems are something to "get over," but I don't believe we even know how to bring them to Jesus until we can tell the truth about our problems. I have often prayed with people who are afraid to tell the truth. They find it so difficult to admit to having real problems or deep doubt. They may be questioning God, or even angry with him, but their prayers still sound very sweet and kind: "God, I just know that you know what's best for me, so I just thank you for all that you've given me, and I just praise you for who you are." It's not my place to judge anyone's prayers, but I think God would be honored with a bit more honesty. He made our hearts, he knows what's in them, so we might as well say it.

At a dinner party in their home one evening, a father asked his six-year-old daughter to offer the prayer before the meal.

"But I don't know what to say," the little girl replied, looking around at the guests.

The father coaxed her a little more, gently pressing. "Just say what you've heard Mommy say."

"Dear Lord," she began, "why did I invite all these people to dinner?"

Do we trust that prayer is the safest place to tell the truth? Do we dare believe that God can hold our hearts and all that is in our hearts? That he fully knows who we are and, even more, who we can become? There is no safer place to begin telling the truth than to the God who made you and loves you. True surrender is to open your hands, lay down your guns, false motives, and strategies, and give the Eyes of love a good look at you. There is no shame at the feet of Jesus. No one can come and pull the curtain back and expose you; the curtain is already open. It's been torn from top to bottom. There is nothing to hide in the presence of God.

Our prayers reveal our shortsightedness and lack of understanding. We pray for God to bring us a friend rather than praying for the wisdom and heart to be a friend. We pray, "Lord, take this struggle away," rather than "Let this struggle change me to look more like you." When we pray and ask God for specific things we want, we are often disappointed. But when we ask for the Lord's will or for his presence, we are never left wanting. God is shaping us by our suffering, and he will not leave us or forsake us in the midst of it. In fact, the opposite is the promise of Scripture, "God is near to the brokenhearted" (Ps. 34:18, paraphrased).

Unfortunately, another promise of Scripture is, "In this world you will have trouble" (John 16:33). In this world, we will face the daily grind. But as the grounds pile up, just know that none are lost or wasted, like our tears. God has a way of using them beyond our wildest imaginations.

Letting the Passionate Love of God Pour through the Filters of Our Lives

The theater was full of laughter, and I was brushing away tears as the credits began to roll. The film, now a classic, was *Mrs. Doubtfire*. There were some fabulous, funny moments, to be sure, but for me it was not a comedy. It reminded me too much of the pain in my struggles as a child of divorce for me to laugh. I left the movie, but the movie never left me.

Robin Williams plays a father who loses custody of his children in a bitter divorce. Desperate to see them, he dresses up as a female housekeeper and is hired by his ex to be their nanny—a job, he soon discovers, that is way more work than he'd bargained for. But the joy of being near his children, playing with them after school, cooking for them—even disguised as Mrs. Doubtfire—is worth it all.

But the end of the film brings the heartbreak even deeper as his disguise is discovered and he finds himself back in court, defending his action before the same judge who had awarded custody to the mother. Daniel Hillard, the father Williams portrays, explains to the judge that one day a week was not enough for him to see his children and that what he did, he did out of love for them. The judge tells Hillman, "That's not love."

The Bible seems to indicate that it is.

The apostle Paul, writing about Jesus in Philippians 2:7, said that he disguised himself and took on the form of a servant, ultimately so that he could be near his children. In Christ, God became one of us to be near us. One day a week (think, church) was not enough for God to see us. So he demonstrated his love for us by becoming a man to serve and save what was lost. Jesus came not "to be served, but to serve, and to give his life as a ransom for many" (Mark 10:45).

Reflecting on this verse, I suddenly knew why this movie had touched me so deeply. Not only was it a story of the incredible self-sacrificing love of a father for his children, it also mirrored so beautifully the greatest story of humankind: that of a heavenly Father's sacrificial love for his children.

God's kind of love is often misunderstood. Much like the judge in the film who called Daniel Hillard crazy, many people hear the story of God's love and don't see it as love at all. But Daniel's children saw it; it was unmistakable to them because they experienced it. Even though the father wore a disguise, his love was real. And his children responded to it because it was free and generous and true.

"Love so amazing, so divine, demands my life, my soul, my all," wrote Isaac Watts in the classic hymn "When I Survey the Wondrous Cross."

In John 4 a woman who went to a well to draw water had such an encounter with the living, ever-loving God:

I had no idea who he was the first time I laid eyes on him. His skin was dark, and he was beautiful. My heart skipped about four beats when he spoke to me. "Will you give me a drink?"

I swallowed hard. He knew that was forbidden. I thought maybe he was testing me to see what I would do, but his eyes gave him away. I knew immediately he wasn't talking about water. Something inside me stirred, and I had to look away.

When I turned back to him, his eyes were still fixed on me. "If you knew who I am, you would ask me for a drink, and I would give you living water."

I couldn't breathe. He was offering to give me a drink. I knew he was a Hebrew, but love can make anything work. The way he was looking at me . . . "Sir," I stammered, "you have nothing to draw with, and the well is deep." My voice sounded shallow, and I felt like a child. "Where can I get this living water?" I asked him slowly, challenging.

He paused, holding my gaze as if it were my face in his hands. "Everyone who drinks this water will be thirsty again," he said as he glanced at the well. "But whoever drinks the water I give . . . will never thirst again."

Each word reached deeper inside me.

Never thirst again. Was he talking about what I thought he was? If he could only know how I thirsted. If he could only . . . he was staring at me, watching my every reaction. "Give me this water so that I won't get thirsty and have to keep coming here to draw water," I whispered.

"Go call your husband and come back."

I had felt like he cared for me, but now he asked this thing of me. Was he mocking me? I stood my ground in shame. "I have no husband," I replied. Tears stung the sides of my eyes.

"You have told me the truth. I know that you have been with many men, and the one you are with now is not your husband." His dark eyes were a sea of compassion as he looked at me with kindness. I was undone. I wanted to say something. I didn't want this conversation to end. I was suddenly afraid he would go away. He was right about my life; he was right about my thirst.

*"You are a prophet." It was all I could think of to say. How else
could he know so much about me?*

God wore a beautiful disguise to be near us. Each day he will
go to great lengths to convince our hearts that a love we never
dreamed existed not only exists, but is available and free. He did
it two thousand years ago, and he is still doing it today.

It Is Well

One Sunday in church, I was very happy to turn in my hymnal to "It Is Well with My Soul." This is a very special hymn to
me. It was born out of great loss, which makes it authentic and
powerful.

I sang the familiar words, trying to take them in as if for the
first time:

> When peace, like a river, attendeth my way,
> When sorrows like sea billows roll;
> Whatever my lot, Thou hast taught me to say,
> It is well, it is well with my soul.

Did I mention this is a very special hymn? The congregation
and I began the second verse:

> Though Satan should buffet, though trials should come,
> Let this blest assurance control,
> That Christ has regarded my helpless estate,
> And hath shed His own blood for my soul.

Trials, surrender, it's all here—the kind of lyrics you hold in
your heart for your whole life. So biblical, so true, so rich.

Fresh-Brewed Adventures

- Spend time in the Psalms, especially when you are
  feeling finely ground. This amazing book reminds
  us that we are not alone in our suffering. Rewrite a
  psalm to apply directly to your situation, and you
  will find some of the comfort hidden there. For
  example, Psalm 61 says, "Hear my cry, O God; listen
  to my prayer. From the ends of the earth I call to you,
  I call as my heart grows faint; lead me to the rock
  that is higher than I. For you have been my refuge,
  a strong tower against the foe." You might write,
  "Do you hear me crying, O God? I believe you are
  listening to my prayer. In the middle of my kitchen, I
  am calling You. I have lost heart. Lead me to a place
  where I can hope in something greater than myself.
  You have been that hope; let me climb to that high
  place again, where I can see and believe."
- Make a date with a hymnal. Borrow one from your
  church and take it with you for a cup of coffee. Just
  sit and read the words of the great hymns. Or if
  you have a friend who plays the piano or sings, get
  together for an hour of worship.
- Schedule a time for stillness this week. Reread the
  section on surrendering through prayer. Bring your
  honest thoughts to God about where you are and
  want you want. Ask for his help to yield your will
  and lay down all of your agendas. Just spend time
  with him who is beyond all time. Give him yourself
  for an hour.

Then the minister of music said the words that always make me cringe, "Last verse."

Last verse? Last verse? Wait one minute, here. You can't skip verses of "It Is Well with My Soul"!

Look at the words to this third verse:

My sin, oh, the bliss of this glorious thought!
My sin, not in part but the whole,
Is nailed to the cross and I bear it no more,
Praise the Lord, praise the Lord, O my soul!"

Yes, there is an exclamation point in the hymnal. You cannot skip this verse.

But he did, and the last verse that everyone was now obediently singing, says "And Lord, haste the day when my faith shall be sight." Inside, I was grumbling.

Wait. You can't haste the day until you have nailed the sin! It will not be well, people. If our sin, not in part but the whole, doesn't get nailed to the cross and we still bear it, no one will be praising the Lord, O my soul. Trust me on this one. So don't hasten the day just yet; go back to the third verse, and nail the sin!

Part of what makes this hymn so special to me is where it starts and where it ends. It's the story of a journey, so each part matters. You can't just skip around or take the parts you like best; you have to take it all for the full return.

So it is with the journey of fresh-brewed life. Starting with every piece of us—all that is lovely, hideous, fun, dry, sinful, beautiful—we authentically surrender it to God. And his love pouring over the grounds of our lives wakes us up to a more flavorful, meaningful, rewarding life than we ever could have imagined. In him, we come to understand the full essence of who we are. We find at last our true identity as deeply loved children. We cry out to a Father who cares, knowing our sorrows are never wasted. In fact, our suffering is making our faith stronger, richer, and more valuable than gold.

Close your eyes. Think of something that makes you smile. Your children in their pj's, a kindred-soul friendship, a delightful painting, a freshly bathed puppy. And smile deeply. Not with your mouth but with your soul. Focus for a few moments on the wonderful things life has to offer to those who pay attention to its gifts. Ask the Creator of it all to guide you on this journey so as not to miss one smiling moment along the way.

2

Encounter
Your Journal

Tuesday, September 15

I feel so uninspired to write today. Do I really have anything to say? I read an amazing piece of writing yesterday, and I felt challenged to write more carefully, crafting each word, like I felt this author had done. This morning I just feel dull, uncreative, and empty. Father, why do I have such overwhelming doubts? I know that you have given me this opportunity to write, and I want to receive it with joy and confidence, but I don't feel joyful or confident. I'm tired and crabby, and I feel completely unworthy to write this book. On days like today, fresh-brewed life feels like an indictment rather than an invitation. I ask for your presence . . .

I started journaling when I was fifteen, on the day I became a Christian. My heart had been filled to overflowing, and there was no one to share it with but God. I wanted to look at the words, feel the joy, and relive each moment. I was afraid I would forget what had happened to me.

I brought my heart to Christ on December 21, 1982, two days

before my sixteenth birthday. My sister, Vanessa, was visiting with us over the Christmas holidays. She had been living with our dad, and we hadn't seen each other in a year or more. We had grown apart. A few years before, she had given her life to Christ; I had given mine to drugs and alcohol.

That particular night of her visit, we stayed up late to talk. We were desperate to try to reconnect somehow, but we spoke different languages. I was cool and distant as Vanessa began talking about the love of Christ, and surprising mainly me, God began a gentle stirring and then a not-so-gentle stirring. At that point her words ceased to be words, and a spiritual earthquake rocked my soul. It wasn't like I even opened my heart; I sort of cracked the door to peep out, and God tore the door off the hinges. His love flooded my life like a swollen river overflows its banks, and everything rose and began to move downstream. I was lost in a new way, caught up in the intensity and passion of the greatest love I had ever known.

I have heard that it takes a new Christian about two years to forget what it was like to be without Christ. Hopelessness is replaced by arrogance. Doubt by simplified certainty. Humility by self-righteousness. I didn't want to forget. The pages of my early journals were full of raw gratitude. I saw so clearly what God had saved me from: myself. He had given me a chance to choose life in the midst of death all around me. At night before bed, I would pull out a blue, cardboard-covered, spiral-bound notebook and pour my guts out on the page. I would write psalm-like odes of amazement and thankfulness for what God had done in my life. My family was in shambles, and my journal became the first safe place I ever found to write about the crazy world I lived in.

It was on those pages that I learned to bring my heart to God, broken piece by broken piece. I learned to pray in my journal, often crying as I wrote. I asked God on paper why things had happened the way they had. I brought him my toughest questions and put forth my requests. Often I would go back and highlight the question or the request when he answered or brought new clarity. Journaling became for me the tangible representation of my relationship with God and my wrestlings with the world around me. Now, almost thirty years later, I still do the

same things. No longer before bed, but as often as I can, I sit with my journal and pen in the presence of the Lord.

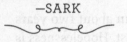

Whatever coaxes us out of hiding, to write, record, and express, is a revolutionary act. It says that we believe our lives count: our lives do count.

—SARK

Countless other women journal as a way of life, and I've found them over the years. Usually, when I find an author I love, it comes as no surprise that he or she has kept a journal for years. One example is Madeline L'Engle. This is what she wrote in *Walking on Water*: "A help to me in working things out has been to keep an honest—as honest as the human being can be—unpublishable journal . . . If I can write things out I can see them, and they are not trapped within my own subjectivity. I have been keeping these notes of thoughts and questions and sometimes just garbage (which "needs" to be dumped somewhere) since I was about nine, I think, my free psychiatrist's couch."

Growing

We have the opportunity to learn from life daily. But so many of us, myself included, miss its lessons and rewards because we aren't paying attention. We barely notice the passages of time. The school bus coming by for another pickup; the notches on the door frame, marking the kids' growth; a beautiful sunrise we never notice, signaling yet another day; the next haircut appointment, marking six or eight weeks that have already flown by. We are not paying attention to our lives when we are merely responding to the tasks required of us. When our souls squeeze out deep questions, like the one we looked at in chapter 1: *who are you, really?* If we're not paying attention, we may try to answer a question like that with our "to do" list. "I'm not really sure who I am, but I'm getting a lot done."

Journaling gives us the opportunity to learn by paying attention. By writing what's happening and what we are feeling and thinking about what's happening, we can look at the pieces and study them more closely. When I open my journal and I haven't written in it for three weeks, that says more to me than someone telling me, "You're too busy." When I see that last entry and realize that I haven't commented on one sunset or written one reflection or talked back to anything I've read in three days, I am aware something must change.

In *Letters to Scattered Pilgrims*, Elizabeth O'Connor wrote, "Journal writing is enforced reflection. When we commit our observations to writing we are taking what is inside us and placing it outside us. We are holding a piece of our life in our hands where we can look at it, and meditate on it, and deepen our understanding of it."

I don't write in my journal just to record. I write in my journal to grow. Nothing else gives me the opportunity to process my life through my own observations like my journal. Because of my dogged commitment to be honest in it, God can work through it, and I can learn and grow from the lessons of life.

Living

This fresh-brewed life, like the life of a Christian, isn't for spectators. It requires our participation, but it is far easier to watch and observe life than it is to fully engage in it. Much of the time, "participating" in life means we need to get our work done. We focus on the task at hand and give all of our available passion and energy to a job or a particular set of tasks. But other times it means taking that day or couple of hours off to drive with the sunroof open or to listen to your favorite music uninterrupted, to rest in the hammock with a glass of lemonade, or to take the kids somewhere you enjoy playing with them rather than watching them play.

If you are like me, you probably spend more time telling yourself why you can't do something than figuring out a way to do it. In this way we rob ourselves of the joy that could be present

Fresh-Brewed Adventures

- Take yourself on a creative date to find a journal. Don't rush! Look for just the right one—it will speak to you. Then find a great pen (you know the difference) and perhaps a small candle, if candles are a sweet luxury for you. Smell every candle until you find one that makes you want to crawl inside it. Now sit down with a cup of coffee, tea, hot chocolate, or your special concoction and just "be" for a bit. Maybe watch people for a few minutes, jot down your grocery list (to get it out of your head), and then open your new journal and make your first entry.
- Get up early in the morning, before anyone gets up. Take your journal and your candle and find a quiet spot in your house. Read Psalm 130. Wait for the Lord. If he tells you something, write it down. If he asks you something, answer him. If he directs you to do something, do it.

in our lives simply by not taking advantage of the opportunities we already have.

This is an edited journal entry about choosing to play over choosing to work—something I wrote in my journal, right in the middle of writing this book.

> I had writing to do yesterday on the book. I had self-imposed deadlines that I wanted to meet, but I was staying as a guest in friends' home. Instead of getting right to work after church, I had lunch with my friends outside on the deck. We didn't hurry through the meal, or worry about the time. I would get to my writing soon enough. Then after lunch, my friend John got out his guitar and we sang songs for a couple of hours. Then it was proposed that we all go to the beach and play. How could I turn that down? Boy, did we play. Two hours later, shoeless, wet, and covered with sand, we marched triumphantly back to our vehicles having swum and played football and volleyball. We did beach calisthenics, laughed at ourselves, and everyone laughed at me trying to throw a Frisbee, until it was dark and we could barely see. The last bits of the day were spent eating coffee ice cream out of the carton in front of a complicated movie.

So I didn't write anything that day. I faced about thirty seconds of guilt before bed, as I realized that I didn't write about having a fresh-brewed life because I was too busy living one!

Should I have locked myself away to write about really living when life was calling me by name to join it? Or should I have trusted that later I could sit quietly with a smile still on my face, a bruise still on my arm from the volleyball game, sand still irritating me in inconvenient places, and relive those memories as I wrote them? Not a tough call, and you know what I chose. I hope I will always choose to participate in and enjoy life, trusting there will be time to write about it later.

The beauty of a good journal is it reminds us to live a life worth recording.

Observing

My journal is my constant companion. It is never very far from my reach. It goes to church with me; it accompanies me on any excursion, fun, or work; it waits for me in the mornings beside my bed or on my desk; and it calls to me in the middle of a hectic day. It is a front porch of solace and retreat when I am tired and weary. It is a battleground of conflicting thoughts, each thought fighting to win the space. It is a stand-up comedy routine of funny observations. It is a newspaper column reporting the details of my life. It is a scrapbook collecting oddly shaped pieces of my experiences. And it is a monastery, where I seek to be still in the presence of God.

We write to taste our life twice, in the moment and in retrospection.

—Anaïs Nin

I write thoughts on what's happening in my life. I write thoughts on what's happening in others' lives. Sometimes I write others' thoughts on what's happening in my life! The main thing is, I'm writing, and when you are writing, you are thinking and feeling. You are processing and working things out. As you put words on the page, you know whether or not they represent you well. You know when you are not telling the truth. You should say so immediately. I might write, "I'm tired, but I am looking forward to this day," then think, *No I'm not looking forward to this day. Why did I say that? I'm being polite.* Then I write, "Why am I being polite in my journal? Who is going to read this? I don't have to be polite. I'm stressed, and this is one more thing I have to get finished before I can get on to what I want to do today." *There. That's more like it.* "Why do I feel so stressed today?

Because I said yes to Karen, when I should have said no. I was trying to be polite again. Okay: Big red flag . . . you have an issue with 'politeness.'" I sit with that big, red flag for a minute and think about what it is to be "too polite." I continue writing, "Polite doesn't mean too kind or too considerate of others. Politeness for me can have an outward appearance of kindness without really being kind. Yuck!"

> **Better to write for yourself and have no public, than to write for the public and have no self.**
>
> —Cyril Connolly

How else can we learn about ourselves if not by forcing our hands to tell the truths of our hearts? Some people hold back in their journals, thinking that someone will read it. They write more "spiritually" than they live, withholding the truth about where they are struggling. One friend made the observation that not being honest in your journal is like trying to cheat on your own health exam!

> The grass in the front yard is brown. It's been too long since the last rain. The consistency of that big, fat star is astounding and maddening. It rises every day, and it burns all day long. Without rain, there is no way for the grass to survive this constant baking. I am brown, spotted, and parched. The sun of this trial, and two weeks with not one drop of rain, have left me scorched and hard. I am angry and hot. My soul cries out for water in this arid place. God, bring rain soon. To the grass in my front yard and to the grass in my soul. I won't make it without you.

Starting

Some of you have been journaling for years, and it is as comfortable to you as your slippers in the evening. But for others this will be a new process. Maybe you have journaled off and on and have never been able to stick with it with any consistency. Don't beat yourself up. Just do the best you can. Different seasons of life bring different opportunities and needs. The worst thing that you can do is to try to make some commitment you won't be able to live up to. Relax. Keeping a journal should never be a pressure; it is an invitation to an oasis, like a quiet time with God. People don't say, "I'm so thirsty. I guess I have to drink water today. One more thing to do." They just run to the water and drink it down.

An Inviting Journal

Search for a journal that is right for you. Buy a couple of different ones and try them out. Some people like lines, and others like no lines. You might like spiral-bound, or more book-style. None of the features of your journal matter except that you like them. Your journal needs to inspire you to pick it up; it should beg to be written in. I love beautiful artwork or creative wording on my journals. When I find a good journal, every time I look at it, my heart jumps a little. I feel a sense of connection with the pages. I feel that writing in such a book will change me in some way. I also like to feel as though it is weighty enough to hold my life. I prefer thick pages that have some texture to them, but I have written in journals that have thin, fragile paper too. Believe it or not, my writing is affected by the kind of paper I write on. It's fun to experiment and see what kind best draws out your words.

An Exclusive Pen

I love pens, markers, colored pencils, and crayons. Marking in your journal with lipstick is permissible (and encouraged), but a favorite pen for your journal is a must. Be careful when you write with a pencil that you do not give in to the temptation to erase. In your journal, you need to keep all the words, even if you think they are the wrong ones. Scratch the words out only enough that you can still read them, and then choose better words—it's how we learn.

Search for a pen that is fun to write with and feels comfortable in your hand. I like pens whose ink flows freely and evenly, so it doesn't slow down my writing. I learned early that ink that doesn't dry quickly can make a mess when you're writing fast and your hand is gliding over the page. Keep your pen with your journal, and designate it exclusively for your journal so it is there when you need it, at a moment's notice. It would be terrible if your great idea, revelation, or invention that will change the world leaves you before you find a pen.

A Window of Time

Time to journal is essential, but try not to neglect journaling altogether if you don't have a large chunk of time to devote to it. Sometimes you can take five minutes and get two thoughts down that will affect the rest of your day. However, when you do have time to spend with your journal, don't rush. It is not a waste of your time to sit with pen in hand, even if you are not putting words down. Switch off "productivity mode" and realize that you are investing in your growth. This takes slow, steady steps. Seeking to savor your life through words or to cultivate gratitude or to learn more about yourself is never a frivolous use of your time. The house will still be falling down around you when you get done, but you will have a new peace about how to put it back together.

A Comfy Place

I don't always get to "create a space" for journaling, but I often try. Sometimes I will light a candle or put music on. Other times I will curl up by the window with a cup of coffee—and listen to the quiet if everyone is gone. I love sitting outside to write when the weather permits. I am always seeking to create an environment where my soul feels relaxed—in other words, I don't write at the kitchen table. I can't finish a sentence, much less write a paragraph there. But just down the hall is the bathroom. It's okay to journal in the bathroom. Anywhere you can find a space or create one that invites you to join it. I will often see more spaces to sit and write if I'm looking for one. It is a great way to set a tone or a mood for your writing.

Complete Candor

When you begin to write your thoughts and feelings, try not to say to yourself, "I can't write that." The "that" is the very thing you must write. You have to silence the critic inside you who will criticize your writing or, worse, shut down your feelings. After you have written a few sentences, resist the urge to go back and read them. Just keep writing; don't interrupt the flow. If you look again at your words, you might want to pick them apart, dismiss them, or rewrite them. Don't give in to this. Your job is to get honest words and feelings down on the paper, not justify them or explain them or make sure they are beautiful—they won't be, nor are they supposed to be. Just write honestly.

Personal Privacy

So many women confess that they don't feel free to write openly in their journals. They worry that their kids will find them or that their husbands will read their entries. It is so important that your journal be for you alone. Short of creating a force field around it, use good communication to indicate this is your book. My journal is off-limits to anyone but me. It isn't a book to be read by others. As mentioned earlier, I don't spend a great deal of time reading it myself. I would never bring my real thoughts or wrestle with ideas on paper if I feared what someone else might think of my wrestling. That's when we end up writing things like, "I know I shouldn't feel this way . . ." or we paste a conclusion on our writing that we don't believe, like, "I guess God is going to work this out," but inside we don't trust this at all.

In fact, if you must keep your journal hidden, do so. I feel sad for women or men who can't write from their hearts without fear their spouses or families will read what they have written. Why should it be a secret? Why shouldn't your spouse be able to read your journal? Because its contents are your thoughts and your feelings—your wrestlings—alone. If you are only writing things that are appropriate for others to read, you probably aren't wrestling deep enough. You

People would ask what I did, and I would say, "I'm a writer!" They inevitably would ask, "What do you write?" When I answered "journals," sometimes they chuckled or smirked, as though journals were less valuable somehow.

—SARK

are always free to share thoughts from your journal, and on some occasions you might decide to read a passage, but it should never be expected or demanded. It's a matter of trust that should never be violated. We all need a safe, hidden place to reveal our doubts, fears, and questions. How can we bring them to God otherwise? We all struggle with our humanity, and if you haven't yet, you may by the time you finish this book. There is no shortcut to dealing with our brokenness. "If we say we have no sin, we deceive ourselves, and the truth is not in us" (1 John 1:8 ESV). Our journals can become a holy avenue to confess our sin, our hopes, our longings, our shortcomings, our triumphs. Sometimes my journal entries are just long rants to God, and I write "Amen" at the end.

Spiritual Direction

I like to have my Bible with me or nearby while I'm journaling. I usually read a passage of Scripture in the morning, and often my first journal thoughts are remarks on or responses to what I have just read. My writing becomes a dialogue with what I'm reading. If something speaks to me deeply, it goes in the journal. Sometimes the Lord will direct me to a familiar passage, like Psalm 23, just to remind me of the still waters that he offers. My Bible is right there for me to find whatever passage he might direct me to. I want to be ready if he speaks, and I want to write down what I sense, as well as my response.

Encountering God

Journaling is not just about writing. It is also about listening. As you have your journal open, write as fast as your hand will go, and listen. But not to that internal editor/critic. If something in your head says, *Don't write that down*, or *You shouldn't feel that way*, you must press through this distraction, or you will never get anywhere. But as you are writing, when you hear the voice of love, let it stop you, and listen with your whole heart. When you are putting down thoughts about a psalm, or even lamenting in Lamentations, keep the ears of your spirit open for the voice of God. Is it any wonder that God seems to speak more when I have my journal out and my heart open?

When we are struggling, he will meet us on the pages. When we are sinning, he will reveal that to us. When we are weeping, we'll hear his gentle words of comfort. And when we write in celebration, we can sense his joy coming through our own.

So the next time you get your journal out, just sit with it for a few minutes. Think about an area in your life that may need God's guidance. Maybe it's money worries; perhaps a wayward friendship is troubling you; it may even be that your spiritual journey needs some attention. Offer a simple prayer, "Lord, I am listening; please speak to me"; then write down what you hear or sense. You may not hear anything immediately. Be patient, and sit. You may hear so much that you can't write fast enough. Either way, listen and then write. Use the silence to try to hear from God, even if he doesn't seem to be speaking. Sometimes it takes our hearts a while to learn to hear him. Keep your Bible handy, not forgetting that he has spoken and still speaks through his Word. Often, when you are in the middle of a struggle, he will direct you to an appropriate passage. Just keep listening.

Encountering Opposition

I hear voices in my head all day long. I've talked to a lot of other women who do too, so I know I'm not completely alone here. Although, I do feel a bit like Ray Kinsella in the classic baseball film *Field of Dreams*. When he said out loud that he was hearing voices, the rumors began to fly; the heads began to shake in disbelief and pity. "Ray is hearing voices in the cornfield." Well, so be it. But my voices, unlike Ray's, aren't calling me to build. The voices I hear try to tear me down. They rise up in me to create fear or to try to convince me I don't have value. I can be minding my own business, just cleaning up the kitchen, and from out of nowhere a voice will tell me, *You should never have let your kitchen get this dirty.* Or, when I sit down to write, the voices come with a vengeance.

You don't have anything to say.
No one wants to listen to you.
You're too fat!
Who do you think you are?
Nothing ever changes.
You say you will, but you won't.

You can't ever say no to chocolate.
If people really knew you . . .
You think you're making a difference, but you're not.
You don't have your own life under control; how can you help
others with anything?

Interesting to me how most women's "voices" are really similar. Probably because they are really just one voice from the same
place: fear. The voices come when we try anything new, creating
doubt about our ability. They come when we put ourselves "out
there" to warn us about what others will think of us if we fail. In
short, these voices will rob every ounce of enjoyment from the
lives we have. Many women have listened to the voices so long
that they live in a constant state of self-disapproval. The voices
can keep us from writing books or changing careers or loving
our children well.

But only if we let them.

Journaling and listening to God are the best ways I have
found to ferret out these voices and loosen their devastating
power. I want to be crystal clear: the negative, judgmental voices
we hear in our heads are not from God. We can't allow them the
freedom to tear down our dreams, erode our courage, and question our worth.

Your journaling in the morning will bring out these voices
with a vengeance. As you begin to write about your longings
and dreams, the minute you put some of your hopes down on
paper, just get ready for pelts from the peanut gallery of fear.
Whenever a woman seeks to move courageously in her world,
clothed in passion and humility, the enemy of her soul is going
to move against her.

So press forward all the more. Write it all down. Somehow,
when I write what the voices say, it takes the sting out. When I pen
the words *You have no worth,* I know immediately that it's not true.

So I ask my journal, or myself, why I feel that way, and then I write, "Your thighs are too big!" I can look at those words and see them for what they are—a fear tactic from the hater of my life—and then I can let them go. On really good days I can laugh at how ridiculous I feel about things. And it's far easier to look at the words written on the page in broad daylight than it is to let them rattle around inside me at two in the morning. I prefer to drag them into the light, where they cannot survive. And to deliver the death blow, I write a scripture, such as "I'm fearfully and wonderfully made," right next to the dark whisper of one of the voices. I look at the words side by side and decide whose voice I would like to agree with.

Directed Journaling

- What keeps you from living your life?
- Write down things you always hear "the voices" say. Try to think back to the past; who said that to you the first time you heard it?
- What would you do differently if you chose not to listen to the voices?

Encountering Creativity

Writing has revealed an avenue of creativity inside me. I first strolled down that avenue through journaling, and a new creative world opened up. I could see shops, restaurants, art galleries, and pet stores, where before there was nothing. Piquing my curiosity, this avenue made me wonder if there were more roads like these. My writing time in the morning became an adventure into unfamiliar towns.

As we turn down the volume on the destructive voices, we are free to turn up the creativity. We cannot write freely or creatively, when we are constantly criticizing ourselves. It's time to explore and dream, imagine and play. God is the quintessential Creator, and because we are created in His image, it must please him to no end when we create. "In the beginning," means before there was anything. He flung the stars into a space where there was nothing. We are imitators of God when we create something from nothing. When there is a blank page and we fill it with words, or an empty canvas and we splash color across it, or we stock an empty refrigerator with food for wonderful meals— we are creating something where in the beginning there was nothing. Granted, creating meat loaf is not quite like creating humankind, but . . . originality reveals our heavenly DNA.

Consider, then, that we are like our adversary when we are imitators. When we eliminate our own creativity merely to copy someone else, I'm not sure that we can be reflecting the image of God. Creativity is hard. On the seventh day of Creation, God rested. He was not tired, but many times after a creative endeavor, we are. Not being God, creativity—or any kind of work, really— takes a toll on us. Staring down at a blank piece of paper is tough, and sometimes the paper wins. But when fear gets the best of us, we settle for imitation.

I challenge you, as I challenge myself, to let your God-given creativity surface. The world needs you. The church needs you. Your ideas, your insights, your colors, your contribution. What you are passionate about was created in you to make something in this life that no one else can make. So make it. Start right now.

Starting my first journal was the cup of fresh-brewed life that woke me up to creativity. Today it is a cup that keeps me awake to God and to myself. Without it, I wouldn't be savoring my life or reflecting on my journey or, frankly, writing this book. A journal is a tool, a flower, a canvas, a safety deposit box, a cup of coffee with a friend. It can hold your dreams, record your life, challenge your thinking, refresh your soul, make you laugh, and redirect your path. That is, if you bring your whole-bean self to the encounter. If you haven't yet started journaling, you're in for a satisfying surprise as the warmth of this cup presses against your lips. If you're an old pro, you already know how rewarding and significant this encounter is. Either way, write your heart out.

Listen to Your Longings

Staring out the sliding glass door into the ocean, she is filled with a strong sense of emptiness. It is her last day of vacation. The trip she'd planned for so long and anticipated even longer, is coming to an end. She doesn't hate her life or her job, yet the thought of returning to both causes great sadness. She'll be at her desk tomorrow, waiting another year for vacation. An ache sets in. She was made for more.

Patty wipes a tear as she hangs up the phone. It is always so hard to say good-bye. Her best friend lives ten hours away, and the loneliness she feels is from more than just the miles separating them. They are soul mates, and Patty yearns for more time together. They had just spent an hour on the phone and could easily have spent more. "What is wrong with me? Why can't I be grateful for the time we have, instead of being depressed that we don't have more?" Unable to muster up the gratitude for what she does have, she puts her head in her hands and weeps. She was made for more.

They have been married for fifteen years. They are still in love and deeply committed to each other. But they are different, and as much as she doesn't want to admit it, there are times when Caroline finds empty places in her soul that Jack can't reach. She tries not to think about it much; she stays really busy, but there are times when she feels like a complete stranger to him. *He doesn't really know me*, she worries, putting words to her fear. As she washes her hair, she tries to send the feelings right down the drain with the shampoo. She was made for more.

Longings. Coming face-to-face with the fact that there are empty places in our lives that haven't been filled. Yearnings. Wanting more than we have: more love, more enjoyment, more passion, more hope, more rest. Cravings. The hope of finding something that will satisfy the rumbling we feel in the stomachs of our souls.

Longings can begin to surface after a number of years in the same job. *Is this all there is?* The same questioning happens in a marriage when a woman realizes that she longs for more love or tenderness than her husband can give. *Is this all there is?* At the dinner table, in the middle of another chaotic supper, a hope for peace and a yearning for rest begin to rise up. *Is it ever going to get any better?*

We were made for more than this world has to offer us.

Our yearnings, longings, cravings, and hopes are telling us something: there isn't enough love, peace, hope, friendship, and intimacy on this earth to completely satisfy us. We will always want more because we were made for more.

This is why we can have a marvelous vacation that satisfies us deeply on one level and leaves us still wanting. It is why we can receive praise and honor from other people and yet still feel insecure at the same time. We were made to run on high-test fuel, and the best we get here on earth is 89-grade octane. It's not that we are ungrateful or greedy. God has designed us to want more out of life, and we won't be fully satisfied until we get it. We cry out to God over this, "How long must I wait, O Lord?" And still we are left longing.

So, are our longings one big cosmic setup for frustration? It seems so, especially if we view them as something to be overcome or eradicated. But if we lean in close to those longings and really listen—they can teach us to understand God and ourselves in a very unique way. Perhaps what we don't have shapes our lives and hearts more than what we have. And perhaps the places left empty, the holes, are part of what it means to be human. If we are somewhat like Swiss cheese, then the holes in us are actually *supposed* to be there—in essence, they are holy (pun intended) places inside us that God has reserved for himself! Our longings identify our real hungers, hungers that will ultimately point us heavenward *if*—and this really is a big *if*—we listen to our longings.

> All my longings lie open before you, O Lord; my sighing is not hidden from you.
>
> —Psalm 38:9

It would be hard to say there was one specific thing that caused me to look more closely into my own personal yearnings. It seems, looking back, that it was more like a long season, during which I became aware of places in my soul that felt hollow and unsatisfied. I wondered if these were new places that had just been created inside me through some event or dissatisfaction, or had these holes been with me for a long time and I was finally able to feel and articulate the ache of them? It would be dishonest to let you think it was a happy season in my life. It brought much pain and sadness up from some very deep, old places. But I can say truthfully that allowing myself to listen to my longings, rather than running, radically changed me. Finding the courage to stare hard into the caverns of my soul fostered a dependency on God that I had not known before.

"Now, wait a minute, Nicole," you may be saying. "I signed on for a fresh-brewed life, not the staring-into-the-caverns-of-my-soul thing. It's dark in there. I'm looking for the light. I want the joy, the excitement, the completeness, the wake-up call. You are talking about pain and lack of fulfillment."

I haven't pulled a bait and switch—I promise. A fresh-brewed life is not a life without pain. First, a life without pain isn't possible, especially a fresh-brewed one (remember the grinding noise of the coffee maker?), but more important, there is life *through* the pain and on the other side of it. Pain can be a wake-up call, and rather than running away or getting stuck in the middle, we can journey through it. There is no pearl without the excruciating grain of sand. There is no treasure without the seemingly endless search. How I wish that weren't so. The easy things don't change us much or produce much in our lives. So let's heed the wake-up call and investigate the caverns. Therein lies the treasure we seek. Longings are the map that will point the way.

Wishes, Dreams, and Longings

A longing is an intense desire for something that is out of our reach. A dream is a strong desire for something that could be within our reach. Dreams and longings are like mothers and daughters—different but related. Wishes are wants and desires. They're still in the same family with longings and dreams, but they are a little more like first cousins. Definitely more common and attainable. Though they're sometimes used interchangeably, longings, dreams, and wishes are distinctly separate, and it's probably better to keep them that way. When we confuse them, it's really easy to get depressed.

Let me try to explain. Say, you think you're *dreaming* of something (remember, a dream could be within our reach), like that perfect husband. Because that is not really a dream but a longing, you could find yourself in a bad place by confusing the two. You'll be waiting an eternity for a perfect husband (literally) and be awfully disappointed in the meantime.

Maybe this will be helpful:

You *wish* for a relationship:

> you *dream* of a husband;
> you *long* for a perfect man.

You *wish* for some cash:

> you *dream* of more money;
> you *long* for enough money to take away all your problems.

You *wish* for more time:

> you *dream* of an incredible vacation;
> you *long* for a place of complete freedom and rest.

You *wish* to be thinner:

> you *dream* of being a size 4;
> you *long* to be the most beautiful woman who has ever walked the earth.

Getting the idea? All of them—wishes, dreams, and longings—have something to tell us about our hearts. Defining these desires is helpful and can point part of the way to the treasure we are seeking. But the same road that leads to the treasure is full of deep potholes of disappointment.

Two Ways We Try to "Manage" Disappointment

When it happens is different for everyone, but you know when you've hit a pothole—it feels like the bottom drops out and you're stuck in a rut of disappointment. You look at your circumstances or your relationships, and you feel a nagging sense of loss. *Is this really all there is?* Deep disappointment sets in, perhaps even resentment. While these feelings are not positive or pleasant, they are the precursors to waking up to our longings. They are the first stirrings, the hunger pangs that tell us we are longing for more. But unfortunately, when we have these negative feelings, we want to run from them. It's common for us to run in one of two directions.

The first direction we might take is toward becoming "spectators" *watching* our own lives. In subtle, or perhaps not-so-subtle, ways, we refuse to fully participate. The spectator prefers to take the turtle approach. She stays busy and keeps all the vital stuff inside the shell, only to peek out every so often to see what's going on. She never pauses long enough to listen to her dreams, so she doesn't have to be responsible to them. Let's be honest—it works for a while. If she doesn't wish or dream, she can't be disappointed. She can't allow herself to even *wonder* what it would be like to plant a garden, volunteer at a hospital, take up watercolors, go to cooking school, earn a master's degree, sing in a quartet, write a book, run a race. *There isn't time. I couldn't possibly. Why entertain the thoughts? They will only lead to more disappointment.*

You may be flipping through a magazine in a doctor's office (because when else would you have time?) and stumble across

> It seems to me we can never give up longing and wishing while we are thoroughly alive.
>
> —George Eliot

photos of a beautiful English garden—and all the steps needed to transform an ordinary space into something spectacular. Something washes over you—perhaps a desire to create something beautiful. You feel it for a moment and then shrug it away. *Who has time for that?*

A friend reveals a painting she just finished and talks about the joy her newfound hobby is bringing, and you find yourself feeling a little jealous. *Where on earth are these feelings coming from?* You've never been a jealous person. Yet you start thinking, *I wish I had done that.* And before you allow yourself to really "go there," you've come up with five reasons why she can have a hobby and you can't.

You're watching a movie that has been filmed in some incredible location, when a powerful yearning stirs your soul. You've always wanted to travel yet somehow never found the time or felt you could spend the money. "Life" was just too full. *But was it really?* Places you have always wanted to visit flash through your mind, and the longing you feel to see and experience them makes you wonder, *Was I afraid? Were those excuses? Did I give up on a dream because it just seemed too hard?* Finally, honest questions bring the tears. But it only takes a moment for the spectator to squelch the sadness. *I would have felt guilty spending the money.* It's not like you couldn't go now. But something deep and familiar rises up against the longing, knowing that you never will.

A reason to hope: even if you become some sort of android woman, you can't completely kill your soul. Dreams and longings have a way of resurfacing. After all, they are in our hearts for a reason.

The second direction we may take to deal with our disappointment is to become "evaluators" *criticizing* our lives and the lives of those around us. We rise above living life to judging life and the quality of everything. The evaluator looks as though she is participating, while staying quite removed from any real experience. She "samples" in order to evaluate, operating like a critic in life. You never ask a movie critic or a food reviewer, "Did you like it?" That would bring stern disapproval. The goal is not to like a movie or enjoy a meal; the goal is to evaluate it based on the individual's opinion of its merit and worth. Yet very little seems to ever have enough of either.

The critic moves in worlds of pleasure but finds very little. She may deny herself nothing but still miss contentment. She hears about the new "whatever," knowing it will be hers to evaluate for those around her. *It's cool, but not really worth the money.* She is on a constant search to find the ultimate experience, the best restaurant, the best pair of jeans, the best vacation spot that will vanquish disappointment in her life. But interestingly, it only seems to create more.

While the spectator stands on the sidelines, watching or working, the evaluator is whining, There is always something wrong with everything around her.

You show up for dinner with friends, and instead of enjoying the experience, you wonder why others aren't noticing what you're noticing and can't get past. The table is too small; the waiter is too slow; the food temperature is off. You point these things out, but more irritatingly, no one seems to care. *What's wrong with them? How can anyone not be disappointed that the food is taking so long?*

You are talking with a friend on the phone who has been dreaming of starting her own business. She's taken the first steps and is filling you in on her progress. Even though you know she's excited by this, you really need to give her all the reasons it's probably not a good idea. *How can someone be so enthusiastic over something that is never going to work?* Your critique is met with some uncomfortable silence on the other end of the phone; then your conversation ends awkwardly. *Why can't I just listen and be happy for her? Am I afraid she might succeed?*

Your home is beautiful. Just the way you've worked for it to be. Of course, not perfect, because nothing is, but good enough for now. Your closet is organized and full of lovely things you've selected for yourself. It's your relationships that seem to be the most uncooperative. Your marriage is either argumentative or silent, and your children think you're controlling. And every once in a while you find yourself wondering how you can have so much and enjoy it so little. *If we sold the house and moved somewhere smaller, could we all be closer? Do I pay so much attention to the details that it separates me from people somehow?* At this thought the evaluator sheds a few tears but quickly criticizes herself. She wipes her tears and schedules lunch with a friend at a familiar lunch place, hoping the food will be better than last time, when her "hot" salad was served ice-cold.

A reason for hope: even if you become a critical snob, you can't completely kill your soul. Did I mention that dreams and longings have a way of resurfacing? After all, they are in our hearts for a reason.

We are masters at killing our own dreams, one way or another. The spectator is no better than the evaluator, even though she may see herself as "selfless" for putting off her dreams. The evaluator doesn't know she's avoiding her dreams by criticizing everything; she simply sees herself as "discerning."

When we operate out of fear, as either spectators or evaluators, we are going to great lengths to avoid disappointment. Even to the point that we extinguish the flame of possibility before anyone else has the opportunity to blow it out. It feels safer that way. Because what if we discover things that we really want and there's no way we can have them? What would we do then? If you said to your husband over dinner, "I was thinking about going back to school," and he made fun of the idea or rejected the notion or felt the decision needed to be made from a financial standpoint, what would that say to your soul? I mean, taking up watercolors is one thing, but what about deeper desires? What do you do with those when they are left unfulfilled? Cooking classes would be fun, but they won't satisfy your dream of having a better marriage. So kill the dreaming, hoping, and longing. Douse the flame before you get burned.

But those pesky dreams and longings—they just don't want to die.

Neither spectators nor evaluators can fully live fresh-brewed lives. Trying to sidestep disappointment doesn't bring the satisfaction that we hope it will. Avoiding pain isn't synonymous with embracing life. Our goal is to become "participators," *engaging* our lives. This means we are on the field playing, not in the stands watching, or on the sidelines criticizing. The participator is the one who not only listens to her dreams but also pays attention to them, to learn something. *Why do I feel this drive to go back to school? What do I really want? What would it free me to be more of the real me?* The participator faces disappointment head-on, recognizing it to be part of life on earth. She listens to her heart, especially when it aches. She will not be able to reach all her dreams or meet her longings, but she will try not to kill them to avoid being disappointed.

> **The tragedy of life is not in the fact of death, but in what dies inside us while we live.**
>
> —Norman Cousins

We move toward spectating or evaluating our lives not only to avoid disappointment but also for another good reason: because we are afraid of pain.

The Fear of Pain

"I want morphine." I walked in to the emergency room and told them so. Loudly. I had another kidney stone, and I wanted to get started on heavy drugs as soon as possible.

"I'm sorry, lady, but before we can give you medication, we

have to admit you to the hospital." Details. I knew the pain that was around the corner if I didn't get medicine fast. I didn't want to wait. Hospitals have these inane rules about dispensing medication, like . . . they have to diagnose the problem before they give you any. I guess it's a precaution that keeps them from treating you for something that you don't really have or from giving you medicine that could actually hurt you. But when you are in intense pain, you don't care if they give you Drano as long as it will bring some kind of relief. Knock me out, take the edge off, send me to la-la land—anything—just make the pain go away.

We don't want to tune in to our longings for the same reason. When we long for something that we cannot have, it isn't pleasant. If we agree to be honest about what we want in our lives, when it doesn't resemble what we have, it can be downright painful. Longings are inconvenient, uncomfortable, embarrassing at best; uncontrollable, revealing, terrifying, and potentially devastating at worst. They interrupt our lives with their nagging and persistence and (we think) keep us from feeling contented with what we have. We worry that they are assassins of our faith and perhaps betrayals of our loved ones.

I want to run away from home. I want my kids to run away from home. I want to eat every last cookie in the world. I want to be Miss America. I want to take a nap. I want to live at the beach. I want to write a best-selling book. I want cellulite-free thighs. I want a beautiful house. I want more passion in my marriage. I want a soul mate friend. I want, I want, I want . . .

This scares us to death.

We're afraid that if we confess that we really want to eat cookies, then we'll eat two or three boxes and never stop. Or if we cry out for more passion in our marriage, then we are going to have an affair. Or if we long to be found beautiful, then we must not be Christian enough. Fear tells us that if we give ourselves permission to confess our longings, there is no turning back and we're inevitably going to pursue whatever we think will satisfy them. So instead of naming our longings and listening to what they would tell us, we try to cut them off. "Get back to work," or "Face facts," we say to our souls.

Now, there is no doubt that a woman who lives only to try to satisfy her longings can bring destruction into her life and the lives of those around her, but that's not what I'm addressing here. I'm seeking to persuade women who have been afraid to tell the truth or be themselves or confess their longings, that there is enormous value in doing so. Because longings are part of being alive. When we try to cut them off, we are trying to keep ourselves safe from life. Longings challenge us to be more than evaluators or spectators; they call us to be participators in our very short existence.

At this point, or perhaps even before now, many women would say, "Die to yourself! This is the *Christian* thing to do." Christians have all sorts of false "spiritual" strategies for dealing with fear and pain. Don't miss my point: we do have to die to ourselves, and that is what the Christian life is about, but you have to live in order to die. Women want to go straight to "die to yourself" before

> There are two sources of unhappiness in life. One is not getting what you want; the other is getting it.
>
> —George Bernard Shaw

they even know what self they are dying to. Then it is not a laying down of their lives but a complete avoidance of pain. That, my friend, is seeking to *save* your life, which is something different altogether. God does not intend for us to cut off our longings or to live in fear of them. He gave them to us. They call us to him.

This is permission to start naming your longings. Write them down. It is important that you identify your longings, so you can listen to what they might mean. Like trying to discover what you're hungry for *before* you start eating. So rather than just eating, you can feel satisfied. You are not giving yourself permission to foolishly try to meet your longings (as if you could); you are simply naming them and seeking to understand their message: you were made for more.

To wake up to this truth will change your life. When you are honest about the places in your soul that ache to be filled, you are right where God can tenderly reach in and connect the deepest parts of your heart with deep parts of his.

Directed Journaling

- What are you jealous of?
- What is someone else doing that you wish you were doing?
- Write about two longings in your life.
- What do you dream about?

The Longing of God

Here is an amazing truth: God has longings too. Although God is perfect, complete, whole, omnipotent, omni-everything, he still longs for one thing: us. Can you believe this? He set up his own universe to potentially leave himself unfulfilled. God's desire is that none should perish, yet he gave us the freedom to choose him as the path to salvation. When we don't choose him, he is not getting what he wants. He is left longing.

Not only is God left longing when we don't respond to him as our Savior, but his longing and grief are very much in the now whenever we place our idols before our relationship with him. He seeks a connective, reciprocal relationship with us, and our choice to direct our passion elsewhere leaves our Creator longing.

When we cry out in the midst of our unmet needs, we are in good company. The best company in the universe. When we bring our longings to our heavenly Father, who is intimately acquainted with longings, he meets us from a place of understanding and compassion. He placed Adam and Eve in the garden, and even before there was sin, there were boundaries. The Tree of Life was off-limits for them. While Eve's temptation ushered in the longing through the serpent's deception, a case can be made that she knew longing before she knew sin, which means our longings in themselves are not always sinful. The lengths we may go to in our efforts to meet them can be, but the longings themselves are not. It's also possible that Adam and Eve never knew longing until after the fall and it came from the separation, but that still would not make longing itself sinful. Can you imagine if Eve had gone to God when she was first tempted by the snake? What if she had wept and said, "I was so tempted to believe that you were not good; I wanted so badly to eat of the fruit you told me not to eat, because I doubted you"? Do you think God would have punished her? More likely, he would have put his arms around her and held her close. Our longings have the power to draw us to God in a passionate, desperate way that nothing else can.

> Jealousy is an oddly wrapped gift that points the way toward where we want to go.
> —SARK

The Longing of *Me*

The longing to be filled, the longing to be known, and the longing for heaven all draw me to him with an intense pull that began the day he made me.

The Longing to Be Filled

I am slow, but one would think that after several decades I would have learned to make peace with "the empty places." But because I have a longing to be filled, I have tried so many times (unsuccessfully) to sate it with food, purchases, and even people. Every time I go to the mall, a million things jump out at me that I want to buy, and the tempter promises me that if I go home with awesome purchases, then I will feel fulfilled. It feels great for a while, but when the bill comes, the longing comes back with it. What am I trying to sate at every meal or with each purchase that is monumentally bigger than wanting French fries or new place mats? My deep, powerful longing to be filled.

This longing rears its head in my life at the table, at the mall, and at the mirror. I suppose ultimately, it is the longing to not have longings. When I eat too much or buy too much or obsess about the way I look, I am trying to fill up my longing for wholeness. I want to have all I need and more. I don't want to feel empty or lacking or less than "perfect."

Physical food is a need, of course; we have to have it for nutrition. But food is also about enjoyment, which makes a Snickers bar a wish or a desire. A $250 dinner at a French restaurant is a dream. But the craving to be completely filled, whole, perfect, and satisfied all the time, this is a longing. I don't want "enough"; I want more than enough. I don't want to eat until I "feel" full; I want to make sure I am full. I want to be in charge of my own filling and not stop until I say "when." Something inside me promises satisfaction if I eat large quantities of chocolate. So I do. For a short time (mainly while it's melting in my mouth) I do feel some satisfaction. But later, when I'm fatter and disappointed, the longing returns, and I feel duped because I wasn't longing for chocolate; it's so much deeper than any food can satisfy. Sometimes, when the desire to feel filled kicks in strongly, I have to remind myself, "This is not a longing for chocolate." Don't use food to assuage the longing.

Emotionally, in relationships we do the same thing. This would be comical if it weren't so destructive. Have you noticed that the law of diminishing returns applies in relationships just like when you sit down to a meal or go shopping? The more you get, the more you want and the less satisfied you feel. Have you ever had this conversation?

WOMAN: Honey, do you like this dress?

MAN: Uh-huh.

WOMAN: Is that a yes?

MAN: Yes.

WOMAN: Then why didn't you say yes?

MAN: I did.

WOMAN: No, you didn't; you said, "Uh-huh."

MAN: That means yes.

WOMAN: Not to me.

MAN: What means yes to you?

WOMAN: The word *yes*.

MAN: Give me another chance.

WOMAN: Do you like this dress?

MAN: Yes.

WOMAN: Now you're just saying that.

Why do we engage in this kind of emotional dance? This seems to be a superficial conversation about a dress, but on a deeper level, it is a strategy women employ to get emotionally filled. Wanting to be full is a legitimate longing, but seeking to meet that longing by manipulating another person to fill it is sinful. And because we need to be filled again and again, it doesn't take very long for those around us who are expected to do the filling to feel set up and used.

The Longing to Be Known

Meg Ryan plays a woman in a "promising" relationship with a man she is getting to know. The two are standing in the produce section when she picks up a pear and takes a bite.

"What does it taste like?" asks Nicolas Cage, the actor playing opposite Meg in the late '90s film *City of Angels*.

She laughs. "Don't you know what a pear tastes like?"

"Yes, but I don't know what a pear tastes like to *you*."

Every woman watching melts, including me.

As much as we conceal and cover up, women long to be uncovered, discovered, and known. As much as we run and hide, we have a far deeper longing to be found—to be really seen and understood. Every woman on the face of the earth wants to be pursued and embraced passionately for who she is. This is the longing that drives us to soap operas, romance novels, and even social networking sites. I am willing to admit I've watched soaps, and I've read my share of trashy novels, but while these stir up longings, they don't come anywhere close to meeting them. I mean, many of the stories or plot lines are written by women! No one knows how to capitalize on a woman's longings like other women. Female writers can create men who will speak our language and meet every need, the kind of men who really can read our minds and know what to do without being told. But these men don't exist. That's not to say there aren't wonderful, godly men out there—there are, but even godly men fall short. If a man is put into a role only God can fill not only is it a recipe for deep disappointment but also it's idolatry.

Like Caroline at the beginning of this chapter, we, too, have places inside us that our relationships don't touch. Each of us has to face the fact that our longing to be known will never be fully met this side of heaven. No matter how much a man can know of us, there is still more to know, more to be embraced. So the yearning continues, and it calls us to look upward.

It is pretty easy to get angry with men about this. Why can't they be all that we want them to be? Why can't they meet our every longing? Do they just not want to? Are there other men who can? If they seemed to try harder, would it help?

Unfortunately, God placed the same limitations on men that he did on women. It's quite a heavy realization for men when they begin to see that they alone can't fill all the empty places inside the women they love. While they can know us and while we can have *incredibly* satisfying relationships, they will never be all that we long for. Men have to come to terms with that truth as well as women and deal with their own longings as well.

The Longing for Heaven

I usually don't spend much time thinking about heaven. In fact, when this longing for heaven surfaced, it was such a surprise that I didn't even recognize it as such. Heaven, to me, was a word for the indescribable, wonderful place I hope to go when I die. It didn't dawn on me that because we hold eternity—or heaven—in our hearts, we would feel a measure of homesickness in our souls all throughout our life on earth.

When all is said and done, no matter how sweet the event, how consoling the moment, there is always a deep longing within us that cuts like a knife. It is a yearning that stirs even when (or perhaps most often when) the air is flooded with sunshine and the sky dazzles us with color and light. Out of nowhere comes this unutterable loneliness that we feel is in no way justified. Yet in the midst of our gratitude for the beauty of created things, we know in our very bones that there is something yet to be given. The emptiness is the mark and reminder of God. By this sense of what is not, we know what is and long for what is yet to be.

I felt this longing so deeply on my first trip to Africa. I was not prepared for the onslaught of longing that was awakened within me. Never had I so deeply connected with a physical place on earth. Travel had always been something I deeply enjoyed, but usually by the end of a trip I was ready to go home. Not so with Africa. I wrote in my journal, "This country has stalked and captured my wandering heart." I felt so very sad leaving. I actually entertained thoughts of running away from home. It wasn't one thing, like the beauty of the land, yet it was beautiful; it was some mesmerizing combination of everything—seeing amazing animals, the relationships, the aliveness I felt in my soul just waking up in Africa.

> When at last I cling to you with all my being, for me there will be no more sorrow, no more toil. Then at last I shall be alive with true life, for my life will be wholly filled by you.
>
> —Saint Augustine

I felt the stirrings of this yearning while I was there, but about three days before I had to leave, it knocked on my door with authority. *What is going on with me? Why don't I want to go home?* I was afraid to answer the door and face the longing—something must be missing that I was experiencing for the first time. And I clearly didn't want to leave it behind.

On the flight home, I opened that door, and an overwhelming longing flooded my soul. The things I had tasted in Africa had awakened a hunger in me that I wasn't sure could ever be satisfied. To be in a place with animals (not dogs and cats—hello?) and feel a sense of the wildness of life instead of the daily familiar workload had been extraordinary. To sit around a big table and enjoy fellowship with people who had lived all over the world had been so exciting. At the end of each day, when the heat started to subside and the cooling began, I breathed in the air of a simpler earth, and I loved it so very much.

And the day I had to leave Africa, I felt more deeply than I had before that I was made for more, that my longing for Africa was bigger than Africa. Because if I could move there, and I did weigh it, by the time I got there, it wouldn't be the same. My time there was a glimpse—it was a taste—of what I now believe heaven must be like, if for no other reason than what the longing promises by its existence in my heart.

But there are days here on earth when the longing just makes me ache.

The Ultimate Longing: The Treasure

The writer in Psalm 42 cried out, "As the deer pants for streams of water, so my soul pants for you, O God. My soul thirsts for God, for the living God" (vv. 1–2). Our longings will point the way to God every single time. Each longing in my life that I have discovered, or that has discovered me, drives me to confront a truth that I may not have confronted otherwise: I am thirsty for God. Desperately thirsty. Just like the woman at the well. Thirsty, still drawing the same old water, but longing for the living water.

Saint Augustine wrote that our souls never find their rest until they find it in God. We were made by him, and our souls are not ultimately satisfied by less than him. Our longings will not let us forget this if we pay attention to them. They will reveal God as their author and as their fulfillment.

It is easy to miss this understanding or even ignore it altogether. I have veered off into sin and missed the treasure on many trips. In the times I have tried to meet that need or longing with something or someone who cannot meet it, I have grieved the heart of God. With my choice I have said, "I don't trust you, God, to fill this longing or meet my need, so I will do it myself."

Because sin masquerades as the promise of fulfillment, we

can be fooled into thinking that the treasure really is the food or the affair, instead of the living God.

Sandra

Sandra came to a women's conference to get a closer walk with God. She got a wake-up call to listen to her longings. She pulled me aside and asked if I would pray for her. "I'm having an affair," she confessed through tears. "I've been married for nineteen years, and I'm so lonely. My husband was abusive for fifteen years. He got help, and he doesn't abuse me anymore, but I'm afraid that I don't love him." Now she was sobbing. I just held her.

"I went back to school two years ago, but my husband doesn't like it. He never asks me about my grades or anything."

"Did you meet the other man at school?"

She nodded. "His name is Jerry."

"Tell me how Jerry makes you feel." Her face softened, tears still rolling down. "Like I matter. Like I'm important." She paused, wiping tears. "He cares about me, and he thinks I'm beautiful, and he wants to marry me."

Now I'm wiping tears away. Not only could I feel her pain; I felt pain of my own. "Sandra, what you want from Jerry is what every woman wants. We all long to be cared for and thought of as beautiful. That's how we were made. And that's never wrong or bad." She stared at the floor, listening. "We get into trouble when we think that a particular man is the one who should completely fill that longing." She looked up at me as I continued.

"But I thought . . ." She stopped.

"We all did." It was my turn to do some confessing. "Every woman thinks she's going to meet the perfect man for her, fall in love, get married, and feel loved and cared for the rest of her life. But it's not enough. Because we were made to want more."

Sandra asked, "More what?"

"More love, more care, more appreciation than any man can give us."

More tears.

"When someone like Jerry walks into your life and turns a light on inside you," I continued, "it feels wonderful." Sandra smiled. "And you start to think, *Here's someone who can really love me.* And as a woman, you have a choice. You can embrace the person who turned on the light, or you can embrace the Light."

"You're saying that what I really want is not Jerry?"

"No, I know you want Jerry on one level, but Jerry will not ultimately satisfy you. It seems so right now, and all you can think about is how much he will, and how he's so different from your husband." Sandra sat, head bowed, tears dripping in her lap. "You're so disappointed in your marriage because you cannot get what you are longing for, and part of you is so afraid that if you let go of Jerry, you never will."

I held her, and we both wept. We cried the tears that count-less women have cried before us and will continue to cry after us. "I want to be loved and cherished." By listening to her long-ings, she was drawn to the right arms. "It's God I really want."

I don't know what happened with Sandra's marriage or whether or not she ended her affair with Jerry. But I know that she encountered God that afternoon, and she would not be the same. She had brought her longings to God, and if she would have let him, he would begin to help her manage them in healthier ways.

God is the only One big enough to hold our longings. When we bring them to him, we have finally found the right place to rest. Emilie Griffin wrote in *Clinging*, "On God we can loose all the intensity of what we are, all the passion and the longing we feel. This is the one surrender we can make in utter trust, know-ing that we can rest our whole weight there and nothing will give way."

Fresh-Brewed Adventures

- Write a letter to God, confiding in him your deepest longings.
- Poetry is the language of longings. Write a poem about one particular longing.
- Take one hour this week and go on a date with yourself. Schedule it on your calendar. Bring your journal and your Bible and go to your favorite coffee shop, sit on your deck, check out a new art store, or take a long soak in the bathtub. Wherever you are, the goal of this date is to create space to be still and listen to your longings.

Learning to Listen

Life is not a paint-by-number kit. The right formula will not "solve" our longings. Painting red in compartment number 22 may be what someone told you to do, but chances are good that your heart is not going to respond when you force it. When Sandra stopped to listen to what she was really longing for, she was open for the first time to the reality that it might not be Jerry. She can own that question fully and seek the answer because it came from her own soul. Longings will not be "fixed" or "solved." Ever. Sandra should never seek to get to a place where she doesn't want to be loved, and neither should we. Our Christian faith is not about trying to kill legitimate longings; it's about surrendering those longings to Christ. Longings are to be wrestled with, surrendered to God, wrestled with again, surrendered again, wrestled . . . You get the idea. Here are some suggestions for "holy" wrestling:

Feel. Get your journal out. Write down some of your wishes and dreams, and in the process identify the longings in them. Allow yourself to feel the pain of where your needs and wants are not being met. Is your marriage all that you desire it to be? Are there disappointments in your family? Is your job satisfying? Listen to what your heart is saying as you ask yourself the questions. Let the answers shape you. What dreams have you given up on? Pay attention, in spite of the hurt. Skip the morphine. Cut up the credit cards, leave the chocolate in the wrapper, and let yourself feel your longings. Feeling keeps our hearts tender and our souls open to be directed to God.

Discern. Is there an area of your life that feels out of control? Is there an unmet longing driving some sinful behavior in response? Dig deep until you find it. Be aware that our greatest temptations always come from good things that we long for. Like Sandra, when we are wrestling with the longing to be known, we are in a prime position to be tempted by an affair. Bad spending patterns or cycles of overeating can be broken by taking our legitimate longing to the right place. Don't be afraid to admit your vulnerability. In our denial, we can be blindsided by the force of our cravings. Learning to discern as we listen can keep us from making mistakes with cheap substitutions.

Grieve. "What am I supposed to do?" I asked my counselor one day. "There are places in me that feel so empty. I cannot fill them up. I know a few sinful things that promise to make me *feel* better, but I don't want to do them because I really do know it won't help and then I'll feel worse. So what do I do?" I was so close to tears. The burden felt so great, and the struggle so intense, that I just didn't know how to let it go.

My counselor looked at me with a knowing that comes from having walked the same road and said, "Put your head on the chest of God, and weep." I couldn't have stopped the tears then if I'd tried. I wept, openly, for a long time. *Put your head on the chest of*

God and weep. Cry a river. The energy that it would take to hold it all together would be better spent on other things, like healing.

When I pulled myself together enough to speak, I said, "I think I'm dying."

He leaned in and responded, "I think you're living." I sat there for a moment. If this was living, I wasn't sure if I wanted life. Counseling is having a safe place to cry.

In *Heart to Heart About Men*, Nancy Groom wrote, "For most of my life I would not grieve, because it was seen as a weakness: Strong women don't grieve. Now I believe only strong women can grieve."

Until we grieve, we cannot be comforted. Until we lay our longings at Jesus' feet, we cannot be met with his presence. Until I come to the end of "longings management"—trying to hold it all together, pretending I'm better than I really am—I can't trust Christ. But when I bring him my crumpled longings, trying to press them straight from holding them so tightly, he will hold them for me and help me straighten them out.

Laugh. Laughter works on the soul like medicine. There are a couple of friends I love going to lunch with. All we do is laugh. We laugh about men; we laugh about our longings and can kind of celebrate them. When we finally get around to looking at a menu, we laugh as one of us invariably orders "one of everything, please, with cheese." Our longings, as we discuss them, create a bond that wouldn't come if we simply stayed on the surface. Real laughter and enjoyment come from going deep and rising to the surface to suck in air. Laughter is almost as important as breathing as it helps us not lose perspective.

Anticipate. Can you recall the feelings of sheer delight you experienced as a child when you thought about what Christmas would be like once it finally arrived? Anticipation is the secret gift of longing. The hope is often greater than the realization. The excitement of a vacation and the energy spent dreaming up plans are often better than taking the actual trip. There is something incredibly powerful about waiting. It keeps our hearts ready and open. Waiting and wondering are treasures to us when we are not overly focused on "getting there." Sometimes not having is better than having, if for no other reason than for the way it makes us feel in the waiting. There can be great contentment in simply longing for something with a peace that trusts in the ultimate fulfillment.

Trust. God has not forgotten you. When God says no to a longing, we are called to trust that his decision not to fully fill it will shape us more than filling it would. These longings are in our lives to shape us by the wanting and to draw us to the real filling. We are becoming more like Christ through this waiting and suffering. I'm not saying that we should choose suffering or love it, but when we can trust that it has a purpose, even if we don't fully understand the purpose, it brings us peace in the waiting.

The happiest women I know are the ones who have spiritual maturity. They aren't giddy happy; they are free happy. If married, their marriages are good, but not everything they ever longed for. They look to God to meet their ultimate needs. No woman is free from disappointment, but these women know how to bring their disappointment to Christ, trusting that he is using it in their lives. This is not something they have told me; this is something I've witnessed and discovered. This is the kind of trust I'm after, finding deep comfort in the fact that despite my circumstances, I can rest because I belong body and soul to my faithful Savior, Jesus Christ.

Hope. God gives us some powerful promises to live by. One such promise is that we are never without hope. He has given us his word that one day we will live in a better place than here. A place where our longings will finally be met. First Corinthians 13:9 reminds us that "for [now we only] know in part." We love in part; we speak truth in part—everything is in part. Can you remember when you were children? You loved as children love, simple and free. It was good, but it wasn't even close to what it would be. And remember when you grew older? You loved as an adult, passionate and committed. But one day—one glorious day—we will really be able to love as God loves. Right now, it's like looking in one of those mirrors that isn't glass. It's really difficult to see anything clearly. You get an image and the general idea, but it's not high-definition by any stretch. However, the day is coming when we will see *him* face-to-face—his glorious face to our less-than-we-want-them-to-be faces. Right now we can only see a dim reflection, such grace for us, but one day we will look into his eyes—the eyes that have seen from the foundation of the world. Now I know in part . . . but soon I shall know fully, even as I am fully known.

All of our hungers, all of our longings, will melt in the power of our Father's gaze when it finds us. Everything we were created to be will be evident, and we will know as we are known. We will *feel* known by God. I can hardly imagine it. We will be whole, filled, and satisfied. All of our pain, every last ounce of our sorrow, any emptiness that we have felt on this earth will vanish like the morning dew. Gone. We will kneel in his presence in a place where there are no tears and where lions lie down with lambs in the kind of peace we can only dream of. The intensity of his love and the encompassing of his embrace will overwhelm us with the deepest joy. As our hearts finally taste all that we have longed for, some will dance, some will weep for joy, but all of us will know that at last we are home.

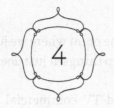

4

Embrace Your Beauty

The terror creeps up my spine before I even get out of bed. I know what lies ahead today. I stay completely still and let the safety of the covers envelop me. Maybe if I ignore it, it will go away. The hard work that will fill my day already drains every ounce of energy in my body. The dread of all the walking, the endless barrage of searching, the tears.

I have to buy a swimsuit today.

What is it about that one purchase that makes my knees weak and my self-esteem plummet? Maybe it's thinking about looking at my body under lights that pick up things the Hubble telescope would miss. Maybe it's the fact that the tops of my legs look somewhat like the surface of the moon. Perhaps it's the futility of trying to make a pot holder–sized piece of fabric cover the square mile of my rear end. Somehow this one activity moves me from a fairly self-confident, mature woman to feeling like I'm back in junior high.

We finally get to the point where we just don't care. We learn to get over it and give up things. It just doesn't matter: I don't ever have to swim again.

I remember an old TV commercial with Cybill Shepherd lounging on a sofa, running her fingers through her hair, saying, "Don't hate me because I'm beautiful." I was ten at the time and didn't hate Cybill in the least. In fact, I thought she was beautiful, and I was kind of sad that she thought women would hate her for that. Now that I've had decades to think about it, and to grow tired of the obsession with beauty in our culture, I'm not so sad for her. From commercials, magazine ads, movies, infomercials, books, and websites—there is nowhere a woman can turn in this world that someone doesn't shove an airbrushed beauty in front of our eyes in order to sell us something. It used to be just products; now it's self-esteem or a better way of life. As if a beautiful face or the perfect body means a better anything. But over time, you begin to wonder.

We are literally pulled in two by our feelings about beauty. We *know* all the right answers about this. We *know* that beauty is on the inside and that we shouldn't pursue it too passionately, but what woman doesn't want to be beautiful? And the church doesn't help much by telling us it's not "spiritual" to spend too much time looking in the mirror. Which just makes us *pretend* that we don't. We dress carefully and intentionally, then respond to a compliment with words like, "This old thing?" We hear a minister with a frowning face say, "Why, you don't think Mother Teresa worried about beauty, do you?" There is much truth in this, but while I want to love as Mother Teresa loved, I'm not sure I want to look like her. We're guilted into rejecting any desire to be beautiful, yet we can't reject it completely. So we stay in no-man's-land, the zone, on the fence, between the lines, pulled in two directions.

The Constant Female Tension

I think *Vogue* is a magazine for skinny women who wear crazy clothes that look too small for them. But I still look at it on occasion.

I think the fashion industry is outlandish, and I wouldn't be caught dead wearing some of that stuff, even to a Halloween party. But I still might try something on to see how it looks on me.

I think face-lifts and cosmetic surgery can be destructive. It makes me mad that women feel the pressure to go to such lengths to hold on to "beauty." But I've thought about having some "work" done.

I rant and rave over the *Sports Illustrated* swimsuit issue. I am angry over the exploitation of women and the way men are so drawn to women's bodies. But I wish I had a body like that.

We pretend we don't care. But we do.

We act as if it doesn't matter. But it does.

We wish we weren't disappointed. But we are.

Why Embrace Beauty?

For some women, beauty has been the enemy. Beauty, or the perceived lack of it, has been the cause of painful rejections, missed promotions, struggles in marriage, or even self-hatred. Given the challenge, let alone the opportunity, to embrace beauty seems about as dumb as trying to spit into the wind. Isn't it better, we reason, to dismiss beauty than to try to embrace something that we fear we don't have? Won't we look foolish if we think we are beautiful when we are not? These were some of my thoughts as I began to think about how negative I had become toward beauty. I was so afraid that I didn't have "it" that I rejected it before "it" or anyone could reject me.

What I miss in my thinking is what not embracing beauty does to me and to my spirit. The more I dismiss beauty as belonging to others, the more I reject opportunities to nurture my spirit, the more I hold my physical appearance at arm's length and try not to care, the more I die on the inside.

Karen Lee-Thorp and Cynthia Hicks wrote in *Why Beauty Matters*, "The more we honor our bodies as us, as intertwined with our spirits, as limbs of Christ, temples of the Spirit, and bearers of God's image, the more we will understand and manage well the power of physical appearance in our lives."

> The most beautiful make-up of a woman is passion. But cosmetics are easier to buy.
>
> —Yves St. Laurent

Seeking to embrace our beauty will wake us up because we have to face all the parts of ourselves that we have deemed ugly and worthless. We have to confront old pains and wounds, and we have to make a choice as to whether we will give way to new growth and life or stay dead. We'll be challenged by what not embracing our beauty does to our families and our relationships. Consider the possibilities: you can learn to embrace your beauty and allow it to bring you joy and delight, or you can give in to the culture's definition of beauty and allow that to rob you of every shred of confidence and enthusiasm you have about who you are.

Linda never looks in the mirror. She showers quickly and wraps the towel around her tightly. She dresses in her closet, away from her husband. She buys clothes that are too big, for fear that something will cling and reveal her ugly shape. She judges other women for dressing inappropriately. She prides herself on her modesty. *So I'm heavier than I want to be*, she thinks to herself. *At least I'm not parading my body around.* She watches her husband constantly to be certain he is not looking

Fresh-Brewed Adventures

- Write a letter to your mother about her beauty and the lessons you learned from her.
- If you've never spent a day at a spa, go for it. Get a massage, a facial, and maybe a manicure or pedicure. Treat yourself to a kindness day, and journal about how it made you feel.
- If you've done the spa day before (not that anyone gets tired of the spa), try a listening retreat instead. Find a spiritual director, and spend half a day with God to focus on caring for your soul.

at other women. She listens intently during sermons about beauty, priding herself that she doesn't struggle with vanity, like other women. *There is one advantage to being ugly: at least I'm not proud.* During infrequent sex, Linda wants the lights off and the covers on.

Jill exercises regularly and wears clothes that fit her form. Jill isn't completely satisfied with her body, but she enjoys her shape and feels attractive. She takes baths and isn't afraid to look at her body in the mirror and survey its contour. She takes time to get ready and usually feels confident about her appearance in public. She spends an appropriate amount of money on nice clothes and enjoys feeling good about how she looks. She sees her husband's eye caught by a beautiful woman, and laughs. "What do you think is beautiful about her?" she asks, really wanting to know. She doesn't feel threatened, as she is secure in who she is. Jill wants the covers off and the lights on.

There is nothing spiritual about hating your own body. So much of what we call humility, and even modesty, is merely veiled self-loathing. Other words for vanity are *airs, arrogance, condescension, disdain*. Of the two women just described, Linda is far more vain and obsessed about her appearance. It is an indirect vanity—invisible from the outside—that holds her hostage. It's a failure to trust God with her body. Jill lives a fresh-brewed life. She tries to embrace her beauty.

I know these women well. I have been both of them on my journey.

Obstacles to Embracing Your Beauty

By placing so much emphasis on beauty, while trying not to at the same time, we put ourselves at odds with how we feel about beauty. We don't gently embrace it; we try to seize it. It eludes us, and we reject it. The longing comes back to us, and we dismiss it like a lover spurned. We have a love-hate relationship with the idea of beauty, created by issues that keep us from embracing it.

We Don't Like Ourselves

Let's face it: most of us don't like the way we look. Incredibly sad and unfortunate, but true. We constantly criticize our appearance and berate our bodies. We don't receive compliments well because we simply don't believe them. We are bombarded by images that make it impossible to measure up, and therefore we cannot accept what we look like.

Consider these statistics from *Why Beauty Matters*: "A 1995 study found that 48 percent of American women felt 'wholesale displeasure' about their bodies. That is, about half of us utterly detest our appearance, while many more merely dislike our weight or breasts or thighs. This self-hatred has spiraled up from 23 percent in 1972 and 38 percent in 1985."

We aren't getting better; we are getting worse. In fact, just projecting the same amount of growth forward to 2015 puts us somewhere in the general neighborhood of *three-fourths* of all women feeling bad about how they look.

The emphasis on beauty in our culture has made self-rejection an epidemic. We believe that if we could eliminate the problems we see in our bodies, then we could really accept ourselves. What an illusion this is. Instead of acceptance, we are drawn into a downward spiral of eating disorders and self-rejecting behaviors that leave us with complete disdain for how we look.

> **The mass media often trivialize our lives and our achievements, narrowing the litmus test of female worth to one question: Does she have dimpled thighs or crow's feet? If so, onto the trash heap of history.**
>
> —Susan Douglas

We Compare Constantly

Most of us could say, "I feel really good about myself until I turn on the television or look at a magazine or watch a movie or stand in the checkout line at the grocery or look at the Victoria's Secret catalog or meet anyone thinner than I am. If I don't do any of those things, I'm fine!"

All women are assaulted on an hourly basis by an invisible attacker: comparison. We have spent years deciding if we're pretty based on how we think we measure up to all the images swirling around us. But we measure ourselves not just against media stereotypes but against every other woman we know. Do you walk into a room and find yourself scanning it for the most attractive women? We watch other women more than men do! *Am I thinner than she is? Do I look like that in my jeans?* Or, *Her hair is beautiful; I wonder what it would take to get my hair to look like that?* How terribly sad to have so little confidence in our own worth as women that we can only find our value in relation to others.

Nothing good ever comes from comparing ourselves, but we do it anyway. When we compare ourselves and feel we come out favorably, we feel proud. When we come up short, we feel insecure. Comparison never leads to humility or compassion or acceptance.

We Listen to Voices from the Past

What events in your past shaped the way you feel about yourself and how you look? Who had the most impact positively or negatively on your sense of beauty? Get out your journal and start to jot things down as they occur to you.

When I was ten or eleven years old, the unthinkable happened: puberty struck, and my breasts began to emerge. What a terrible inconvenience. Breasts were not useful to me at ten, nor were they desirable. They didn't help in climbing trees or sliding into second, and as far as I was concerned, they were overrated (I still kinda feel that way). Well, my mother decided it was time to shop for a bra. Could there be anything more humiliating than missing playtime after school to go to Sears with your mom to shop for some uncomfortable harness that you didn't want to wear anyway? When my mother told my stepfather where we were going, he contributed these words to my memory bank: "She doesn't need a bra; she needs Band-Aids!"

I was mortified.

I may not have wanted these new growths on my chest, but I wanted to be made fun of even less. Band-Aids? Now I had to be concerned with the fact that I might not be normal. Maybe I would never fully "develop," as they called it back then. Like a photograph that you don't have to pay for when you pick up your pictures at Wal-Mart, I would be "underdeveloped." That's major at eleven years old. I still remember it. The message I heard was my breasts were small, and that was funny. It is a message that I have carried with me all my life. In fact, the other day I commented to a friend, "One great thing about having small breasts is that nobody wonders if they're real!" I have learned to laugh, but that laughter was born of pain, and it still affects how I see myself.

We Are Held Hostage by Pain

In *The Face of Love*, Ellen Lambert reveals an event in her childhood, her mother's death, that radically altered her view on beauty:

> I understand now that the transformation of myself from a beautiful child to an ugly one is so distressing to me because deep down I have known all along what it was: a response to an overwhelming loss. When I look at those early photos of myself I realize that what I am seeing and responding to so positively is the way delight and security inform a child's whole physical aspect. Looking at the photographs closely, I realize how many of the details I read as "beauty" can be referred back to the love at the center of that charmed circle . . . all those outward-reaching, confident gestures, of a body at peace with itself in the world. And so it comes to me now, with the same rush of understanding, that what I am responding to when I look at the images of myself sitting awkwardly on someone else's porch, with the wrong dress and the wrong hairstyle, and features which seem to have lost their right relation to one another, is the enormity of the loss that wrought such a change . . . I didn't just *become* ugly; my ugliness in those later childhood years was a response—in a

sense *the most powerful response* I could make—to the turning upside down of my whole life.

I was on a plane when I read her story. I had to close the book and cry. When my parents divorced and my life was turned upside down, I felt the deepest awareness of loss I had ever known. But I had no words for it. My body, posture, hair, and disposition responded for me. Very little was "right" in my life after that. I, too, have pictures of me looking completely out of place, wearing the wrong thing, in some "other family's" home. On the plane I opened my journal and wrote, "Pain always finds a way out. Like water seeking low ground, pain worked its way through my body, affecting and afflicting everything about the way I looked until it found its way out." Beautiful children are the ones who know they are loved and accepted. A bright smile, confidence, and warmth are born in the soul of one who feels loved. Without love and acceptance, any hope of beauty is missing too.

> Genius is of small use to a woman who does not know how to do her hair.
>
> —Edith Wharton

Karen Lee-Thorp spoke for all of us when she wrote, "I didn't need people to tell me what colors I looked best in so much as I needed people who gave me reasons to wear happy colors instead of sad ones."

We Put Our Beauty in the Hands of Men

Did you date guys who respected you, or did you have to "prove" yourself and your worth just to try to keep a relationship? It's amazing what one or two early, bad relationships can do to our self-concept. "You should cut your hair like this." Thank you. "You should wear more dresses, not jeans so much, like guys do." Okay, got it. "Why don't you smile more? You're too serious."

I tried hard to be everything that any guy wanted me to be. For the record, if you feel horrible about yourself, dating does not help. I was so hungry for love and acceptance that my self-worth was a small price to pay for any tidbit of affirmation. So when a relationship ended, as it always did, I spray-painted "Defective" on the wall of my soul.

Many women live with men who hold impossible standards for what they feel their wives should look like. This can be devastating to a relationship. While we cannot change our dads or husbands or boyfriends, we must try to get untangled from unrealistic standards. Learning to embrace our beauty is a journey each woman must begin for herself. It is not a destination she should seek in order to please someone else.

Beauty Means Control

I have come to know many women for whom weight is the litmus test of their self-worth—and the worth of others. As they see women around them who are in control of their weight (never mind how poorly they may manage it), they bestow on them the "ultimate compliment" of envy. *There is a woman who is in control of her life.* And without realizing the limitations of such judgments, they in turn believe that any overweight woman is a failure. The incredible qualities that may make her successful and beautiful in the eyes of her children, husband, or even God are overlooked or, worse, dismissed as less important.

In our American culture in particular, what a woman weighs instantly classifies her either as one of those who have their "act together" or those who "need to try a little harder." It simply is not enough to be smart, hardworking, talented, or committed if you aren't in shape as well. To have the gifts that can navigate a corporate merger or handle with patience the five o'clock feeding frenzy of twins is of little worth if you don't also have buns of steel. Unfortunately, a woman who works hard all day long but doesn't wear a size 6 can still be thought of as lazy.

Susan Douglas addressed this thinking in her cultural commentary book, *Where the Girls Are*, pointing out that our society places inordinate value on body parts, like perfect thighs. We treat them as an achievement to be admired because "they demonstrated that the woman had made something of herself, that she was the master of her body and, thus, of her fate. If she had conquered her own adipose tissue, she could conquer anything."

Beauty Means Money

Shouldn't the kind of beauty that some women possess naturally be enough reward in itself? Interestingly enough, the workplace gives more "points" to beautiful people than to those it deems otherwise. Employers demonstrate their belief in this system with significantly bigger paychecks for attractive workers. Studies begun in the '80s that continued through the '90s indicated that people perceived as good-looking were making at least 5 percent more than their average-looking coworkers. I have no reason to believe this has changed. If anything, the difference in pay has probably increased since the study was conducted. I don't notice our culture placing less value on attractiveness; in fact, there are days I wonder how it keeps increasing, but indeed it seems to. So how others rate your looks affects your perceived level of success, and it directly affects what you get paid.

Like Mother, Like Daughter

When your twelve-year-old, ninety-pound daughter starts obsessing about her weight or wanting to go on a diet, something is wrong. It may not be completely the world's fault. Yes, girls do go to school, and they are bombarded by the same media that we are, but do we model love and acceptance ourselves? If we cannot embrace our beauty, we'd better get ready to see our daughters struggle to do the same. I am always surprised by women who want their daughters to have a strong sense of their beauty and yet are unwilling themselves to work on showing them the way.

A woman named Julia told her story in *Why Beauty Matters*:

> When I was very young, I thought that my mother was beautiful... Then one day, I saw her look in the mirror and grimace at her reflection. I was confused. I asked her what was the matter and she said she looked "ghastly" without her makeup. I also remember her complaining that she had nothing to wear even though I thought her wardrobe was vast and magical. By the time I was six or seven, I realized that my beautiful mother did not think she was beautiful at all. That made me sad—and it made me sad to see her not eating in order to get thinner. I remember wondering why someone as beautiful as my mother would think she was ugly. And then why did she tell me I was so pretty? What did it mean to be pretty? Was I pretty enough to look in the mirror and like what I see?

I, too, thought my mother was the prettiest mother in the world. I loved watching her put on makeup or curl her hair. I remember sitting on the floor, just staring up at my beautiful mother as she got ready to go out. But she could not appreciate her own beauty, and she deflected all compliments. Over the years it completely discounted my ability to believe her when she told me I was beautiful. I learned how to deflect compliments too. I thought she was a poor judge of beauty because she couldn't recognize her own.

> **If thigh reducing creams really work, why don't they make your hand smaller?**
>
> —Rita Rudner

Our daughters need to see us embrace our beauty. As mothers we are not evaluated by our children on our stylishness or our figures. It is so important not to criticize yourself in front of your daughter or dismiss her compliments to you. When you model self-hatred, your little girl will model it too. When you diet, she will want to diet, too, because you're showing her how much you value being thin. She will never listen to your words; she will only look at your life.

Directed Journaling

- Make two columns on your journal page. On the left write the names of your family members who communicated to you that you had value. Underneath their names write some of the things they said that stand out in your mind. Was there anyone who told you that you were beautiful? Any special aunts or uncles or grandparents? Write their words in your journal.
- Now think through some of the negative messages you received. On the right, write who in your family caused you to question your worth? Was there a sibling or parent who constantly criticized your appearance? Was your father able to express his love to you? Write out prayers of forgiveness.
- For most of us, the second side of the page will be a lot easier to fill in. Not only do we remember the negative far more than we do the positive, but chances are good that there wasn't as much positive.

Four Ways to Enhance Your True Beauty

Uncovering the things that went into shaping our early concept of ourselves is helpful to the degree that it enables us to move on to the present. There is no way to embrace a sense of the beauty that God has given us if we don't look back for clues about why we believe what we do about ourselves. If we are plagued by doubts from the past or have trouble receiving compliments, we should take a closer look at the factors that shaped our present opinions.

1. Be Kind to Yourself

I don't know why we treat ourselves so poorly. Even some of the nicest women I know can be so critical of themselves. We say mean things to ourselves that we would never dream of saying to anyone else. We call ourselves stupid or ugly. Or how about when we disappoint ourselves? *If you were a better Christian, you wouldn't have done that!* Could you imagine saying that to someone directly? So why do we think it and say it to ourselves? *When are you going to lose some weight? You are so fat! Look at yourself!* If a friend ever said any of these things to me, we may not even be friends anymore—yet I've said those things to myself and worse.

Learning to be kind to yourself is about softening that harsh voice that you use inside.

If you are unhappy with your weight or any area of your life, don't beat yourself up. It solves nothing. Shaming yourself, for whatever reason, will not bring about change, In fact, creating a cycle of shame and guilt can send us in the opposite direction. It leads us to think things like, *Well, you've blown it so badly anyway; you might as well just give up trying to eat better or start tomorrow. Yeah, tomorrow is a good idea.* In the area of weight loss, shame starts me on a cycle of putting more pounds on. Whipping myself into shape used to produce some temporary results, but now it only makes me tired and sore. Try accepting where you are. Try trusting that your next decision can be a good one. Try nurturing your soul and thinking kinder thoughts when you want to criticize yourself.

2. Listen to the Longing

There is another Nicole Johnson. I first discovered this when she won the Miss America Pageant in 1999. I remember thinking, *This is just great! All I need in my life is to share the same name with one of the most beautiful women on the planet.* No pressure there. It was a passing thought, really, until I was being interviewed on the radio. The host of the show asked me what it felt like to be Miss America. Let's just say the moment was, um, well, um, uh, ahem . . . awkward. So, if you bought this book thinking I had been Miss America in 1999, I hope I haven't disappointed you.

The truth is, I felt kind of disappointed, and I wasn't sure why. It wasn't as though I ever wanted to be Miss America until I had to say to the voice on the other end of the phone, "I'm not Miss America. So obviously I'm not who you think I am." I've never won a beauty pageant, and truth be told, I've never entered one and never would—but in that moment I didn't feel like talking about it at all. I really just wanted to hang up and cry.

Wanting to be beautiful is a longing. We can't reject the longing to be lovely; it's important. We should listen to it and discern what it is saying to us. We cannot be dominated by it or try to meet it in inappropriate ways, but we must acknowledge that it exists and that we are drawn to it. Like every longing, it is telling us something. We were made for more. We are daughters of Eve. We were created in God's image, and we are beautiful. But we are fallen, and we live in a fallen world that cannot value beauty as God has created it. In the hands of the world, beauty becomes only external, about a face or other body parts, instead of about the whole woman, heart and soul. Therefore, we are left longing.

I tell the story sometimes about the confusion between me

and the other Nicole Johnson. Many of my friends know that it's happened on several occasions, and unlike the first time, I'm learning to laugh about it now. I don't dismiss the longing; I listen to it, and in the midst of it, I can smile.

So one day, I received this e-mail from a friend:

Is this Nicole Johnson's e-mail? Is this *the* Nicole Johnson? The best-selling author, the popular speaker, the long driver, the sweet singer, the marathon runner, the interior decorator, the stay-up-late, get-up-early, never-met-a-challenge-she-didn't-like Nicole Johnson? Is this the stay-the-course, dwell-in-the-Word, raise-your-hands-and-sing Nicole Johnson?—or is this just Miss America?

I laughed out loud. Such kind and generous words that brought a different perspective to the whole incident. Sheepishly I thanked God for the Nicole Johnson he created *me* to be. I also thanked him for the gift of a friend who saw more in me than I'd been able to see in myself.

3. Discover the Secret

There is no beauty in makeup. Expensive clothes will not make you beautiful. The secret lies in being an alive, awake woman with something to offer the world. Namely, yourself. Real beauty is less about your actual face and more about the heart that beats underneath it. It is less about the trendy shape of your eyebrows and all about the light in your eyes. Less about the shape of your nails and more about the openness of your hands. Less about the length of your legs and more about the bounce in your step. Real beauty must radiate from a place no makeup can reach, no tweezers can shape, and no bronzer can color. As you participate in your life with a compassionate, warm smile and a generous spirit, you are beautiful.

Living a fresh-brewed life will bring out your beauty because it reveals more of the authentic you that is beautiful. As you embrace the things that are beautiful about you, this will inspire you to embrace the beauty around you. You'll begin to see it more and appreciate it more deeply. You'll notice the fall leaves or the spring flowers; you'll pull over to see the sunset or notice a beautiful piece of music. Whenever you seek to wrap your arms around the beauty of what God has made (including yourself), you are opening like a flower to the sun, saying an enthusiastic yes to God, and it will warm and color your life.

4. Embrace the Lover of Your Soul

Many women believe that God is silent on the subject of beauty. Maybe because the church has been silent, maybe because we have to stop long enough to listen to what God is saying, or perhaps we sense that God, like many men, simply feels uncomfortable being a part of the discussion. For whatever reason we've thought that God seems absent in our beauty discussions, the fresh-brewed truth is that God doesn't care. He doesn't look at beauty the same way we do—trust me: he knows beautiful, and he created and loves us as we are. His love and care aren't affected one ounce by the size of our blue jeans, the way our nose slopes up or down, or how much dental work we've had or haven't had done. His love isn't diminished if we wear the wrong dress to the party, have no skill (or time) to apply makeup, or hate exercising. God simply loves us. Which also means that if we decide to get in shape or find time to take a shower or learn to wear colors that look nice on us, God still loves us. We haven't "gone up" in his eyes or improved in his estimation of us. He just loves us, the same as he always has and always will.

Have you let that truth into your soul? I mean, really let it in, way down deep? That if anyone ever laughed when you wore the wrong thing, it wasn't God. If any boy ever said you were fat or

made fun of you, God didn't like it either. He is the one, maybe
the only one, who has never criticized you or belittled you or
made fun of your appearance in any way. He has loved you since
you were born, and he loves you right now as you hold this book.
If you could see his eyes looking at you, you would notice that
his whole face radiates love. He is the designer of your form, and
he is the first one who said, "She's beautiful." His tone was kind,
and his words were true. You can believe him.

In Luke 7, "a woman who had lived a sinful life" (v. 37)
brought an alabaster jar to the feet of Jesus. I am certain it was
the most beautiful thing she owned. It represented her very life.
At his feet, she poured out all her longings, all her struggles, all
her attempts to measure up, all her sinful efforts to get filled.
She poured it all out at the feet of the One she believed could love
her differently. She finally found the right feet. And Jesus was
moved. The Pharisees were embarrassed by how honest she had
been with Jesus (they always will be, by the way) and wanted
him to send her away. But Jesus would not. He recognized in
her a heart of longing. He could see her flawed attempts to meet
those longings. For the first time in her life, she didn't seek to fill
herself up; she came to pour herself out. And Jesus forgave her.

And he will forgive us too. All of us who have brought the
alabaster jar of who we are to the wrong feet. We have tried to get
filled in countless ways, many of them sinful. We have brought
our pain to people who could not ease it, though we desperately
hoped they could. There is only one pair of feet that can receive
our poured-out lives. The ones with the holes.

If you have given up on your outward appearance out of fear
or self-rejection, now is a great time to begin healing. A special
fragrance or a new pair of shoes can show your soul an act of

kindness. Clothes don't define you; they reveal you. Makeup isn't meant to cover anything up; it is intended to help you look as alive as you feel. Start allowing the living, breathing, feeling you to encounter the world in an authentic way.

There is freedom from the tyranny of beauty. That freedom is not found in being its slave or in rejecting it all together. If you could see me right now, writing, you would laugh out loud. I'm sitting at my computer with wet hair in two-day-old clothes. Not a pretty sight. But we live by faith, not by sight. I feel kind of beautiful because I am alive and awake and fully participating in my life. I feel free because I am loved and cherished by God, and I know how to love and cherish those in my life. I am thinking kind thoughts about myself as I am, not waiting until I get all the cellulite off my thighs or my skin is clear or my breasts have magically increased two sizes. I'm free to embrace the beauty I have been given by God, in whose embrace I've been set free.

5

Interview Your Anger

Almost twenty years have passed since the following story occurred, yet the event remains clear in my memory for the significance it still holds.

It all started with the statement I feared the most: "You're just like your mother!"

I felt the words like a physical blow to my gut. I couldn't respond. I grabbed my keys and walked out, slamming the door behind me. I didn't go far, maybe two blocks. I was already crying, but I pulled over to the side of the road and sobbed uncontrollably. I gripped the steering wheel tighter and tighter until my fingernails cut into my hands. I was so angry, the pain felt good.

The history of my relationship with my mother was rough, to say the least. To hear those words by someone close to me was one of the most hurtful things that could happen.

I couldn't stop crying. "It's not true!" I couldn't be like my mother. If I had become like my mother, who was angry, I felt my life was over.

I was so tempted to keep driving. But to drive on would not only prove the words right but also would destroy any hope of change or a better future. Either way, I felt I'd lost.

I didn't keep driving.

Facing the Woman in the Mirror

That evening became the first step of what would become a life-long journey to work on issues in my life. I made a commitment to face myself truthfully. And, that's where I started.

Anger is so hard for women to admit. We are afraid of it. We don't want to be labeled "angry." There is an ugly stigma attached to women who are angry. Men are considered powerful when they are angry. If they are leaders in business, or even in the church, they are seen as forceful or strong. But women who are angry are often labeled *shrews, nags,* or *men-haters,* who are irrational or out of control. We get called the ever-popular "b" word. So, we get angry silently. We try to hide our anger. We take our hurt and frustration and bury them, like a dog does a bone. We have holes and tunnels beneath all the rooms in our houses. When our husband or friends sense that they might have stepped on the soft ground of some buried anger beneath the surface, they may gingerly ask, "What's wrong?"

"Nothing!" we snarl, as we slam things around, convincing no one.

Anger is never buried dead, says Gary Smalley. It's always buried alive. It has a way of digging out, especially when we don't want it to. Many women would rather be labeled anything than "mad." So when anyone asks us if we're mad, we usually lie. We stuff, bury, hide, avoid, deny, close up, and shut down. And then, lo and behold, we find ourselves standing in front of the dryer in a rage or reduced to tears because we can't find the mate to the black sock! Or we blow up in the grocery store and say horrible things to the clerk because there is no more Chunky Monkey ice cream. This would be the time to ask a few important questions: *What is going on? Where is this coming from? Are my anger and frustration really about socks or ice cream?*

No. Real "ice-cream disappointment" is brief. "Sock anxiety" (even during PMS) is *not* filled with rage. When we find ourselves intensely angry over the little things, or things that should be little things, it's time to wake up. Anger is a signal to heed carefully. When the CHECK ENGINE SOON light comes on in your automobile, there's something you need to pay attention to. Tears in the grocery store are telling you something. Yelling at your children over Legos means *Listen, your soul is sending you a message*: CHECK ENGINE SOON.

But what do you check? Like a good mechanic, your job is to look under the hood and do some investigating to find out what is causing your light to come on. But many women treat their souls the same way they treat their cars, paying little attention until something breaks down. We don't really care what's going on under the hood, as long as the car is still running. We hope our problems will simply right themselves. And if they don't, perhaps we'll make it to the auto shop before everything falls apart.

> Anger is a tool for change when it challenges us to become more of an expert on the self and less of an expert on others.
>
> —Harriet Goldhor Lerner

Harriet Goldhor Lerner, in her amazing book *The Dance of Anger*, wrote, "Anger is neither legitimate nor illegitimate, meaningful nor pointless. Anger simply is. To ask, 'Is my anger legitimate?' is similar to asking, 'Do I have a right to be thirsty?'"

By holding internal debates over whether or not we should be angry, we hold to an illusion that we are wrestling with our anger or solving it while actually we are doing nothing. Most women want to get the anger out of their lives, but they don't do anything to bring it about. They talk about it but never change their patterns of relating or do the work under the hood that is required to find out what is wrong.

Surveying the Situation

I propose using the interview process. When your son or daughter comes running into the room, crying that "I'm-in-pain" cry, you immediately look for blood. If you don't see any, you start the interview process. "Where does it hurt? Try to breathe; can I see it? What happened? Can you put any weight on it?" The answers to these questions are important because they tell you what your next move should be.

The interview process is critical because the source of our anger is often hidden or obscured. A surface issue may be causing your immediate anger, but when you have a major blowup or when there is rage, something else is bringing fuel to the fire on the surface. You have to be a tough interviewer. Sometimes it may take a counselor or a friend to interview you to try to get to the source. Someone has to be able to ask you hard questions, like, "If you are sitting in your car, entertaining thoughts of leaving home, knuckles white, crying out of control over the thought of being like your mother, can you see that something is terribly wrong?" My counselor, Ken, helped me see that. He also searched with me to find the source, the underground fuel dump, that fed much of my anger.

The Source

My mother left my father when I was five years old. One summer morning, my mother dressed my sister and me, braided our hair, and packed us in the car with my brother for the long drive to visit MaMa and PaPa. I vaguely remember being excited about

the trip and the weeks of summer we would spend with them.
I had no idea we would never go home again. My short, five-
year-old life in another state was completely erased. I would not
return to the bedroom I knew, in a house I had loved, next door
to friends I had made. I would never live with my father again.
We moved into a two-bedroom apartment when I started second
grade. My mom was working to support
three children. My father would make
the seven-hour drive between our states
as often as he could, and we would have
joyful reunions and agonizing good-byes.
There is no way to explain divorce to a
child. It is pure, undiluted pain.

> Don't be afraid to
> take a big step if
> one is indicated.
> You can't cross a
> chasm in two small
> jumps.
>
> —David Lloyd George

I can picture in my mind the day the
battle between them began. We were sitting on a park bench when Dad asked us
if we wanted to come and live with him.
I thought by saying yes I could bring our
family back together and curb this raw longing for my father.
That longing wreaked havoc in my world as our case went to
court. Mother and Dad fought for our loyalty. They were the ones
divorcing, and we were the ones on trial.

"Who do you want to live with, Nicole?" I was high up, not
sure if I was standing or sitting, when the question came from an
attorney below me. From my place on the witness stand, I heard
words coming out of my throat, but it was not my voice. I had
lost my voice. I had been prepped for weeks, and I knew what I
was going to say, but it was not my voice. My voice, my real voice,
would have been one long, woeful wail, like some kind of animal caught in a torturous trap. I simply said, "My mother."

She won and Dad lost. The truth is, we all lost. I lost more in
my soul than I'd ever been aware that I had. I went forward as a
negative from that day on.

Dad made it clear to me right after the trial that he had a new family now to care for. He was sad about my decision but awkwardly said it would be best for him to move on, to just "start over" with his new family. The lump was too big to swallow. How could I object when I had made my choice? A choice that haunted my nights for decades. A choice that created anxiety around making any decision of consequence for fear of disappointing someone. A choice that wasn't a choice at all, but a setup by two adults focused on their own agendas.

Mother and Dad became bitter enemies. I would not see them together again in the same room, with the exception of the mandatory pickups and drop-offs, until my college graduation. The next twenty years would see me on the "witness stand," being forced to choose at every crossroad. Mother would declare that if I wanted Dad to come to something in my life, like my birthday party or my high school graduation, then she simply would not be attending, but I was free to choose him if I wanted. Dad would be kind but would clumsily try to explain why he would not be able to make it to whatever he was being invited to.

Nothing I could do could change or fix my broken family. Good grades, good manners, good intentions all fell short. I cried out in my own little-girl ways. I "performed" to try to be "better," but nobody heard or saw. I stood on the outside of my life, watching. I had no voice after that "choice" I made. I had spoken for all time, and nothing else seemed to matter to my dad or to my mother. And when my mother married for the fourth time, I was just starting high school. Speech came out that day, but it was still not mine: "Congratulations."

When I gripped my steering wheel two blocks from my house and wailed like that wild animal, I broke the silence. I finally found my voice. When the rage subsided, I spoke words in a tiny, wounded, six-year-old voice that had been soundless for twenty years. "God, help me," I whispered.

Asking the Right Questions

Psychologists tell us that anger is made up of fear, frustrations, and hurt feelings. So when we find ourselves angry, we need to start the interview. *What am I afraid or fearful of? Where have my feelings been hurt? Why am I frustrated?* Good questions will take us right to the heart of our anger. If we answer them honestly, they will help define and clarify the real issue. Which probably isn't the trash, or the television, or the laundry. It is more likely something closer to feeling neglected, unloved, or rejected that ignites because of the trash, the television, or the laundry. If it is neglect you are feeling or rejection that you are afraid of, once you unearth your feelings, it becomes possible to deal with them.

However, if you don't know where your anger is coming from, there isn't a lot of hope in dealing with it. Those around you walk on eggshells because they don't know when you're going to blow. If you say you are angry about the laundry piling up, but you feel something so much deeper, there could be a fuel tank underneath it. So much so that when your son forgets to put his clothes away before practice after four reminders, he sets a match to the tank, and it explodes.

The next time you get angry about the laundry, take a few minutes to conduct an interview. Ask yourself, *Why is this hurting or frustrating me?* "It hurts because I don't feel appreciated. I feel frustrated because I'm the only one doing the laundry around here." You have given yourself the opportunity to transform your tone and demeanor from a warrior on the warpath, to a softer, more tender woman who feels alone and underappreciated. If your feeling alone still causes you rage, continue digging until you find the fuel tank. Keep the interview going until you get to the soft place of hurt. Looking back, when in your life did you feel unappreciated and alone? Chances are good those feelings didn't start with your son, but he is getting the fallout from them. Underneath our anger is usually a wounded heart. It is far easier to embrace and comfort a wounded heart than a raging Indian with a tomahawk. If we stay in our anger on the warpath, we will perpetuate the feelings of isolation and abandonment that made us angry in the first place.

Getting Help

"Why are you afraid to be angry?" my counselor asked me.

"I'm not angry," I answered, somewhat flatly. I would rather lie and still maintain my posture that Christians can handle hard things and not resort to the "lesser" emotions, like anger. Lying is much more spiritual.

"If I'm angry, I guess that means I'm like my mother, and I cannot be that."

"If you are angry and you don't deal with it appropriately and you are going to let it destroy your relationships, as you are doing right now, well, then you are like your mother."

"Oh."

I didn't think I was afraid to be angry at all. I actually thought I was angry enough, thank you. But Ken was right. Underground behaviors, like kicking someone under the table or furtively glaring, belong to people who are afraid to be angry, people who try to couch it or hide it. I spent so much time stuffing and denying my anger that I wasn't paying attention to all the ways it was coming out. I thought I was hiding it, but it was showing all over, like a two-year-old trying to hide having eaten a chocolate cookie.

My anger with Mother probably began as deep hurt when she left Dad. But because I was five years old, I can't remember much. I certainly didn't have the words to communicate it back then. But fear and frustration grew as I got older and felt afraid to say no to her for any reason. I did what she told me to, but I resented her in my heart. By the time she married for the fourth time, I'd lost a lot of respect for her. Still, I couldn't stand up or communicate honestly. I still had no voice. I felt powerless in our relationship, and that created more anger.

When I came to faith in Christ at sixteen, our relationship was better for a while. I swept my feelings under the new rug of faith and just tried harder to deal with her hurtful ways. I would "forgive" her in my heart without ever saying a word—thinking I was honoring her as the Bible admonished.

Then the day came that my strength ran out. I couldn't put up with any more. I was an adult, and I felt punished by my mother during a particularly difficult holiday visit, and I cut off our relationship. I didn't understand at the time that by cutting her off, I would become more like her.

As I started counseling on a regular basis, I would tell Ken certain things I thought about my anger and why it could be affecting me this way or that. Then he would say something like this: "You're so grown-up and in control. You've told me what you think, but where are your feelings? Where is the little girl right now in your grown-up world of thinking?"

> Lord, grant me the serenity to accept the things I cannot change, the courage to change the things I can, and the wisdom to hide the bodies of those I had to kill because they really hacked me off!
>
> —Anonymous

The moment Ken asked me anything about that little girl inside me, I would start to cry from some deep place. Shyly, she would come. A little, six-year-old girl who could only weep. I had to go back to my past to find her, and I had to help her to heal. I understand now why many psychologists believe you can't heal what you don't feel. And although I felt pain as a little girl, I had no way to communicate that pain or feel the loss that it brought. In Ken's office, I shed tears for a lost childhood, for parents who didn't love each other or didn't know how to love me. I identified with the psalmist who wrote, "Day and night tears have been my food" (Ps. 42:3, paraphrased). The previously silent little girl suddenly had a lot to say. She'd never had words before. There are no words for divorce when you are six. Just pain. I realized how completely out of control I felt as a little girl. I couldn't stop anything from happening: the divorce, the custody battle that pulled my heart in two, or the new families that both my parents tried to build with new spouses. I not only felt helpless and powerless, I was. And I made a commitment somewhere deep in my soul that I never wanted to feel out of control or powerless again.

Where Does It Hurt?

Women will do almost anything to keep from feeling powerless, including hurting others so we don't have to feel hurt ourselves. We develop a hard exterior over the top of the wounded place. If anyone hurts us in any way, they deserve to be punished. I call this "hard hurt." The woman who has hard hurt reacts like an animal, letting a fear of pain lead her behavior. She will bite you if you try to help her. Hard hurt pushes people away and, on some occasions, even seeks to hurt in return for help. A woman who wants to heal must move through the hard hurt to the pain underneath: the tender hurt of the soul. Tender hurt can be soothed, calmed, healed, and dealt with.

The interview process is the only thing that moves me from hard hurt (*Stay away from me*) to tender hurt (*I'm afraid*). Sometimes I have to feel around a bit inside to discover the wound. "What is really hurting me right now?" Without allowing myself to find the real hurt, I am quite capable of biting whoever is closest, whether or not that person actually caused the pain. Anguish can make us do things we wouldn't do under less stressful situations.

Fresh-Brewed Adventures

- Take a long walk with your journal. Find a spot along the way to pray. Ask God to show you any area of your life in the past that may have caused anger or rage inside you. Listen to what he says, and write down your memories from any particular incidents that come to mind. Follow up on those notes at another time by writing down your feelings around the circumstances you've described.

- Start an anger log in your journal. Anger is like a submarine: it's hard to track because it stays submerged until something brings it to the surface. Keeping a log of the surfacing will uncover some patterns you can pay attention to.

- Write a letter to someone you've been angry with, or are still. Don't hold any intention of sending the letter, just use it to clarify your feelings and write it all out. Interview until you find the hurt or the frustration or the fear, and write about that.

- The next time you get really angry, try exercising. Take a time-out and go for a run, get on the stair stepper or treadmill, or just walk around the neighborhood twice. You will be amazed how some physical exertion can clear your head, release tension, and help you calm down, so you can better solve the problem.

Sometimes we can't even find the tender hurt underneath. The hard exterior has covered it for so long that we can't get in touch with the original hurt. Keep searching. Keep interviewing.

Keep pressing until you begin to find it. It's so important for your healing.

If a leg bone is set properly after a break, it will heal well. Your body, designed by God, is always healing itself. New bone and marrow cells grow, and with proper care the broken leg will be as good as new. It's a miraculous thing. But if the bone is not set properly and is just left alone to repair itself, or if it is set too quickly, the miracle of healing can become a disaster. Growth becomes your enemy as it seeks to heal and reproduce new cells on a broken place, causing more pain and sometimes even deformity.

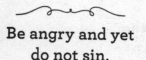

Be angry and yet do not sin.

—Jesus

Some of us are limping around on wounds that are decades old. I was. We may not even think of them as wounds anymore because they don't even really hurt, but they are not healed. Healing at a later stage like this is a hard treatment. The bone must be re-broken and then set right to heal correctly. Proper healing can be the difference between limping and dancing. It also makes the difference between anger and joy.

Directed Journaling

- What is your earliest memory of being angry? What is your most recent memory of being angry? Can you determine how they might be related in any way? Why not ask someone close to you what they see about the two events?

- When have you ever been dishonest about your anger? Why do you hide it? What do you think you may be afraid of?

Re-breaking the Bone

I wrote her a letter. It went through four drafts, and the process took months, but I remember the day I sent it. I put a stamp on it and dropped it in the mail slot (I told you this was a long time ago) and knew there was no turning back. I also remember that day because I felt love toward my mother for the first time in a very long time.

In the letter, I invited my mother to come to meet with Ken and me. My words were simple and honest about the road I had been on for the previous years. I told her about my counseling with Ken and that I had come to a place where I felt we ought to at least get together and talk. I wanted to have a relationship with her, I wrote, but I needed a new model. What we had in the past was not going to work for me anymore, and if she would be willing to meet with us, we could try to forge a new way together.

I really had no idea how she would respond. I was pretty anxious for a couple of weeks. I had no intention of calling, so I just had to wait. And pray. I asked God to work in her life and heart as well as in mine, and I affirmed that I would trust him regardless of her response.

I held the envelope a long time before I opened it. I looked at her distinctive handwriting and wondered what it would say on the inside. She had not responded to me on fancy stationery; she had written on pages from a pad I recognized as one she kept by the phone. It wasn't a long letter, but I knew it was hard for her to write. "Of course I'll come," her cursive read. "I want a better relationship with you more than anything . . . I understand it will be painful for both of us. I do feel if it eases your pain, it'll be worth it to me. I love you, Mother."

I cried as I read her words over and over. She was coming to meet with me on my terms. I was so proud of her. There was no anger in her response to me, and she was more open than I could have imagined she would be.

On June 3, 1994, she met me at Ken's office. It was a time to re-break the bone. I told Mom my version of how my childhood had gone and that, even if she didn't agree, I wanted to share it with her. Over the next three days, we wrestled and cried. Our viewpoints weren't always the same. Mother had reasons and hurts that I had never known about. We held each other. She asked for my forgiveness, which I gave freely. I asked for her forgiveness, which she gave generously as well. The whole process was remarkable for us both.

The bone had been reset straight. We were tired and sore, but we trusted that healing would come. Like putting our relationship in a cast for a while, Ken helped us set new boundaries going forward that would let our relationship grow straight and strong.

Two Good Questions

Anger can make us rush to action, and that is rarely wise. If we can sift through our feelings before we speak or act, we will be far less likely to wound others. We will get our needs met more often than not when we respond calmly and without anger. The clearest position to move from is one that has been thought through and prayed over rather than rushed into. Instead of "Ready, fire, aim!" taking the time for an interview can help us shoot straighter.

1. "Am I Compromising Myself?"

Many times, when I find myself angry, it is because I have not been clear about who I am. Either I didn't stand up for something that was important to me or I didn't communicate well, and a misunderstanding resulted. Knowing this doesn't always make the anger go away, but it helps me understand where it is coming from and reveals my part in it.

In *The Dance of Anger*, Harriet Goldhor Lerner admonishes us, "In using our anger as a guide to determining our innermost needs, values, and priorities, we should not be distressed if we discover just how unclear we are. If we feel chronically angry or bitter in an important relationship, this is a signal that too much of the self has been compromised."

Anger can help us define our boundaries. If my mother calls me at 7:00 a.m. and I am frustrated when I hang up because she woke me, then I have a choice. Either I communicate that I don't want to be called that early, or I let it go. If I simply ignore my feelings or am afraid to ask her not to call before 8:00 a.m., then I am setting myself up to be angry with her over my failure to define myself.

Anger can also help us define our priorities. Many times, when we have not done the work of identifying the things that are important to us, we will feel unknown and potentially angry about this. If we can get clarity about ourselves, more often than not, people will respect that clarity. But it's unfair to think someone should respect a priority that you have not even respected them—or yourself—enough to define.

2. "Am I Mad at God?"

If we believe that God is sovereign, then ultimately our struggle with anger comes back to our relationship with him. *Why did God let these things happen? Why didn't he stop that person from abusing me?* Or, *How come he wouldn't help my parents stay together?* Or, *Why would he allow my mother to die when I was young? Surely if God is sovereign he could have made my life turn out better.* These are valid questions and concerns—so valid, in fact, that we must ask them boldly. We can't let them rattle around in our souls, believing the worst about God, without letting them see the light of day. If we try to put "God anger" anywhere but with God, we will annihilate people. Our husbands cannot handle our "God anger." Our children will not stand under the weight of it. Good news: God *can* handle it. He isn't afraid of it or of us. When we bring it to him and wrestle our questions to the ground with him, it will not destroy us or hurt God. But to stuff those questions, or pretend we don't care one way or the other when we really do, has a way of hurting not only us but also those around us whom we'd like to love.

I don't have a problem with anger!

- Are you critical of other people?
- Are your kids constantly doing something wrong?
- Does your family frequently ask, "Mom, why are you mad?"
- Have you broken anything in anger?
- Does your husband feel praised by you?

The Continuing Story

Seventeen years of new growth have taken place on the "bone" of my relationship with Mom. We have something we never had before: a real friendship. In 1998, when I began to write *Fresh-Brewed Life*, I told her I was going to tell about my journey. I didn't ask for her permission, but I did let her know I was going to write some of our story. She told me to write from my heart and not think twice. "If God can use my mistakes to help others, write every word."

Well, I'm sure you can surmise that I did write every word. But including the hardest parts without telling you a little about my mother today would no longer be fully accurate. Nor would it allow you to see the healing and growth that have taken place in her life. She is not the same woman I grew up with. Her faith came alive after decades of dormancy and changed so much on the inside. Her spirit opened in countless ways as she surrendered areas of her heart to God. I have since come to understand more of the pain in my mother's journey, pain I could never understand as a little girl. But as a grown woman, God has given me compassion.

She is in the thirtieth year of a committed marriage. She is a loving grandmother and an active member of her church. My mother is living proof that it's never too late to grow. Where I had lost respect, God has restored it. We still have our issues, as we always will, but we have sought to be honest with each other and keep short accounts. No more hidden fuel tanks and no more broken bones.

Before *Fresh-Brewed Life* came out in 1999, I sent her this chapter to read. She called me when she was finished. "You didn't need to send it to me," she said.

"I know," I responded, and smiled. "I wanted to."

"You're a good writer." She paused. "Parts of it were hard to read . . ." She took a breath. "But it was good to be reminded how far we've come."

I agreed. I hung up the phone and sat in stillness, at peace. Healing.

It is impossible to live in this world and not be a little bit angry, especially if you are searching for hope, love, and real, fresh-brewed life in a world that doesn't have very much to give. This universe is badly broken and leaves us feeling so unfulfilled at times. Coming face-to-face with that truth can drive us to our knees, and it can infuriate us. Facing the pain underneath our anger will enable us to embrace life from a tender, open place. Living honestly and authentically is what we are after, and that does mean getting angry sometimes. But by God's grace, we can deal with it appropriately. We can ask the right questions, raise the hood, and tap around a bit. When you hear something skipping or find something broken, take the time to set it right. Seek to find any underground fuel tanks, and drain them dry. Let the healing begin.

6

Savor Your Sexuality

savor: to delight in: enjoy

—Merriam Webster's Collegiate Dictionary, 11th edition

I have been stalling. This is not an easy chapter to tackle.

Just the thought of this cup of fresh-brewed life may send many women running for their footed pajamas. Very few areas in our lives hold as much potential for shame and hurt as our sexuality. Even if you had a healthy environment in which to grow, explore, and come to understand the context and the gift of sex—no one gets it completely right. No one has a relationship that is baggage free. Especially in this sex-saturated, intimacy-starved culture, the media's messages alone are enough to create questions and difficulties for us. Many women live "under the covers" in quiet desperation. Lost somewhere between longing and fear, engaging in sex but wondering if it's all God intended for it to be. We watch with one eye open as television, movies, music, and magazines portray and define sex with mystifying simplicity, while we struggle privately with its complexity. Often, church doesn't seem the appropriate venue to discuss the subject openly, although with safe small groups emerging, many are finding help there. But when we have been wounded, or abused (one in every four of us has), the bewilderment and pain surrounding our sexuality intensify. Our questions go unanswered.

I can remember sitting in silence in women's groups while they chatted and giggled about sex on a superficial level, wondering to myself if anybody was telling the truth. I couldn't understand why I had such trouble and pain, so I looked at the floor a lot. I can remember listening to sermons about sex (looking back, I can say, *not very good ones*) and trying to hide a few tears because I wasn't a "better" wife—never understanding (along with that pastor) the heart of the issue.

I won't set you up by asking you to try to become the sexual goddess of your husband's dreams. I won't shame you in this area that holds enough shame already. Instead, I hope to explore some of our questions together and, in doing so, release some of the leftover shame that still lingers in our bedrooms. I hope to encourage you to open the door of your soul and let in delight, true delight, in how you were made.

As we are growing and waking up in new ways, our sexuality is bound to be affected. You may have already noticed a few changes, just from experiencing some of the previous cups of fresh-brewed life. When we begin to wake up spiritually and emotionally, it can't help but affect us sexually. Because each of us is a whole person, the things that affect us in one area of our lives usually spill over into other parts.

How we feel about our sexuality finds expression in many areas: our dress, our speech, the way we walk, how we engage others, and especially how we treat our bodies. Understanding and embracing our sexuality, initially, has very little to do with anyone else. We first seek to find our inward footing from being created in the image of God and choosing to believe (along with

God, I might add) that his creation is good. Only then are we free to choose how we will express ourselves as we follow his design.

Even when we are free, with God's help, to choose how we express ourselves, as women it isn't easy. We are bombarded by magazine covers (because you don't even have to open them to be assaulted), television commercials, and movies, to just name a few. Messages and images coming at us daily are too numerous to count. Then factor in all that we hold inside, our values and our faith, our issues from childhood, and there's no doubt that this is one confusing, complex subject.

How do we get it right? We want to be sexy, but not too sexy. We want to look good, but not too good. Each of us wants to be a godly, beautiful, smart, talented woman who cooks, cleans, ministers to the homeless, bakes her own bread, has passionate sex, changes diapers like a pro, teaches a Bible study, works from home, never yells at her children, wears a size 4, and lives in a picture-perfect house!

How is it possible that in striving to be everything, we end up feeling as though we're nothing? Perhaps because "everything" is an illusion. "Everything" is an idol that will break our hearts. We must choose intentionally and wisely from our list of "everything" and then accept it as *enough*. As sad as it is, we often choose more externals from our list of "everything" than internals. And if I can communicate one thing from this chapter to tuck away inside your heart, it's this: the internal qualities of you are the foundation for sexual expression.

The Inside Versus the Outside

If we are made in the image of God, the *imago dei*, and we hold that very image inside us, then the biblical language of our bodies as temples of God begins to make sense. Maybe like a master architect, God developed a set of plans for our temples. Because of this broken world, no one can implement the plan perfectly. In fact, the finished product may not look exactly like the blue-prints (or the fingerprints) of God, but the design is close enough to hold his image. The outside of the temple doesn't matter nearly as much as the treasure it was designed to hold. Therein lie the ultimate beauty and worth of the creation. A barn could hold the most exquisite treasure, or a mansion could be vacant and cold. Focusing on the outside alone is a trap, while seeking the treasure on the inside reveals the truth.

Not that our culture values mansions and barns equally. This is where much of the confusion arises. The culture, and most people (probably men and women equally), don't understand or recognize the *imago dei*, so they elevate the mansion over the barn. They judge the inside by the outside alone. Without the ability to see the treasure inside, or a faith that reveals it, a person's only option is to focus on what he or she can see on the outside. If a man or woman can't read, what choice would that individual have when looking for a book but to focus on whether or not he or she likes the looks of the cover? Scripture tells us that while man, or humankind, focuses on the outward appearance, God looks at the heart (1 Sam. 16:7).

If you're reading this book and have yet to choose a mate, please pay special attention to this section. When it comes to deep and lasting love, as well as the expression of that love though intimate connection, the treasure inside us is what is shared, exchanged, and enjoyed. Our bodies play a part in this exchange, no doubt, but to elevate the body above the soul in this intimacy is to miss the greater joy, the deeper connection and satisfaction.

Two things to consider in changing our perspective:
1. Men are attracted visually, so they have typically been the ones to value the mansion over the barn. They are designed to respond to beauty but are tempted to settle for the glit-

ter over the gold, not only because of the way the glitter is
promoted and sold but because the gold is harder to find and
takes more searching and effort on their part. Many men are
simply not willing (for too many reasons to mention here) to
do this kind of work, or they don't think it matters all that
much.

2. Women are attracted relationally. We are designed to respond
   to strength and security but are tempted to settle for physical strength over strength of character. Or we find ourselves
   drawn to someone with money over someone who under-
   stands real wealth. Many women are fearful of being alone
   or lack the strength to reject any man, regardless of how they
   are treated by him. Unfortunately, some women place value
   on style over substance because they simply can't tell the
   difference.

Because both men and women have placed a higher value
on the face than the heart or on the wallet than the soul, we
share responsibility for the damage this
has done. Repentance in some form must
take place on both sides for real healing
and change to occur. But I want to consider here what we have done to ourselves
by focusing so much on our appearance.
This outward focus (I'd like to use the
word *obsession*) has wreaked havoc in
our lives. This belief that we are what
we look like has created insecurities that
manifest themselves in everything from
eating disorders to self-mutilation to obe-
sity and manic exercise, as well as trust issues that run deep. I'm
not saying we created these issues all by ourselves. We had help
along the way. It would be tidy, but not healing, to blame others

> Sometimes I
> wonder if men and
> women really suit
> each other. Perhaps
> they should live
> next door and just
> visit now and then.
> —Katharine Hepburn

for this. But we can't if we want to get well, because somewhere along the way, we chose to believe the lie or to accept someone else's way as the truth.

My purpose in raising this is not to focus too much on the past or criticize us for believing this lie in the first place. My intention is to encourage us all to stop believing it now. We may not have known how to live differently at eight years old, but we can live differently today. We can choose to place more value on internal qualities than on external appearance. We can adjust our vision, and keep adjusting, until we clearly see the *imago dei*, in ourselves and in those around us and, most important, as it relates to intimacy, in the soul of our spouse.

Just Hold Me

"Would you just hold me?" may be the worst words a woman could say to a man. If they aren't number one, they rank right up there with "I just want to be friends" and "I'm just not in the mood." Even if a woman's heart is tender, these words feel like rejection to a man. In these cases, the word *just* stops him in his forward motion, and that's frustrating. *Just hold me—no sex. Just be my friend—no sex. Just not in the mood—no sex.* If the message is *no sex*, a man often becomes unavailable emotionally.

This creates a challenge, not only because the words "*Would you just hold me?*" must be said at times but also because there are instances when it feels to women as though sex stops real intimacy in its forward motion. Our masculine counterpart can become focused on his goal and set out to achieve it, leaving his feminine partner feeling abandoned. If sex sends a message of no intimacy, women can become unavailable emotionally as well and even pull away physically. Many women simply "go away" during sex. They paint the living room or review shopping lists in their minds because nothing is engaging their souls.

You can see the way the cycle begins. Men and women may desire the same level of connection and closeness, but because we are designed differently, we pursue it differently and experience it a little differently. This requires us to work together for a level of mutual satisfaction that is enriching to the relationship.

There are times it feels it might be easier to fly to the moon.

Things we do to avoid sex:

- Stay too busy
- Pick fights
- Pretend we are sleeping
- Have headaches
- Eat too much
- Focus on the kids
- Try not to look attractive

What do women really want from sex? Like everything else about us, it's complicated. But I think it's safe to head in this direction: women desire a body, mind, and soul connection. Even when we settle for less, it is less than honest not to admit we value emotional closeness and intimacy. We want to feel united with someone on more than a physical level. Which is why we often just want to be held. We want to feel safe and secure and embraced in our souls, not just in our bodies.

We don't want to be looked at; we want to be seen. We long to be *known*. Women want to be sexy, but there is more: we want to be passionate. I'm not implying that women don't give up on passion and settle for trying to be sexy—but it's a bad trade. Passion is so much richer and deeper because it comes from who we are. Our whole-bean essence. Passion can reveal the image of God inside us. You can't wear passion. You can't see passion until you encounter it in a person's being.

Women long to be known. Many references to sex in the King James Bible are centered on this "knowing." I kind of get a thrill reading these words, "[He] knew his wife" (Gen. 4:1, 25; 1 Sam. 1:19, and others). One of our deepest longings has the possibility to be touched during physical intimacy, if the emotional and spiritual pieces are in place. We don't want to be lusted after or used, although too many women will accept these as substitutes. We want to be embraced wholly, as we are, for who we are.

Girls in our culture are caught in the crossfire of our culture's mixed sexual messages. Sex is considered both a sacred act between two people united by God and the best way to sell suntan lotion.

—Mary Pipher

We hunger for sex to be a wonderful part of this complete knowing, but not the sum.

It was hard to hide my shock one afternoon at a marriage seminar where I was performing when a woman came up to me and said, "My husband and I are divorcing. I am signing the papers tomorrow. But you know, we've always been good in bed." My shock came from her candor as much as her confession. We are wired differently, obviously, but she proved this point. It takes more than sex, even good sex, to make a marriage what it must be to survive. Her husband must have known how to meet her needs in bed, and perhaps vice versa, but because their physical intimacy didn't translate to the soulish intimacy of love and trust, their marriage was ending.

The goal of a good relationship is to communicate and connect deeply. Obviously sex, especially for men of few words, is perhaps the best way to do this; however, for women, it doesn't satisfy us at the deeper level if it becomes the only way. We must continue to be held close. There must be healthy patterns of relating to each other in nonsexual ways. There must be a dogged commitment to deal with any destructive issues that persist in the relationship in order to maintain love and trust.

Waking a Slumbering Sexuality

Savoring is going to look different for every woman, but let's go back to our definition of *savor*: "to delight in: enjoy." What would it take for you to find more delight and enjoyment in sex? Half joking, some of us might say: a new husband, a better body, fewer kids, a different past, clean sheets, an uninterrupted hour . . . But what about accepting ourselves, heart, soul, and body? What about freeing our spirits to be more playful? Or getting reacquainted with our senses? Because these were, and still are, important elements to me in my journey, let's take a closer look at each.

Cherishing Your Body

It's not very appealing to remove the fig leaves when you don't like what's underneath. I've spent a fair number of years now working on this issue of accepting my body. Problem is, our bodies change. Just when we think we're almost to that point of acceptance, something happens to change everything. Pregnancy occurs or exercise routines get interrupted or the holiday stuffing takes its toll or another birthday brings more gravity challenges as the years add up. Which is why we can't wait to accept our bodies until we like them—we'll never get there. We must lavish a little of the divine love we've been so generously given on our sagging or tight, baggy or strong bodies—unconditionally. Only when we make peace with the pieces as they are can we offer them without embarrassment or fear.

Now, this doesn't mean that you can't make changes or

shouldn't try to firm up some of the jiggly parts if you want to. But don't lose the perspective. We mustn't change to get love; we can only really change because we are loved. When we take care of our bodies because we care for them, the changes that occur are lasting. When we crash diet or try to abuse our bodies to produce "results," we don't get the kind of long-term change and acceptance that can bring satisfaction.

Stopping short of attending some Kathy Bates-like support group from the film *Fried Green Tomatoes*, where everyone pulled out mirrors and looked at their own private parts, I had some work to do. Something had to give. I wasn't comfortable with the way my body looked, so I began to pray for God's help to accept my body or for the courage to change it. God gave me a little of each.

I wanted to find a home in my body. I'd checked out because I didn't like what I saw. I would glance in the mirror quickly, if at all, and hardly ever without the "leaves" of clothes. I felt alienated and uncomfortable in my own skin. As part of an assignment I gave myself, I would stand in front of the mirror and ask God to help me find something beautiful there. Even if it was just my eyes or my feet, probably the two things I was most familiar with and the two things that seemed to reflect some kind of truth from my soul. When I found one thing I could be grateful for, I would let myself walk away from the mirror. Sometimes I stood there for what seemed like hours, until I found one thing. After several times of doing this, the "one things" began to add up. I'm not saying that I began to like my body as a whole at that point, but I did find things that I could focus on and believe in. My confidence grew, and some of the old insecurities began to fade.

I committed more gently to taking care of myself. I started running to get into better shape. I started slow and didn't run far, but it made me feel great. I would come home after a run, get in the shower or the tub, and stay for a while, just to focus on my body. I was getting a new shape from running, and it was important for me to notice and acknowledge this. I was starting to respect my body for the way it carried me and for the strength that it was gaining. I bought a few bath products for what had become my time at the end of a run. I wasn't by any objective standard "in shape" or living in the body I had always wanted. I was simply taking care of myself inside and now out.

Rediscovering Delight

I wanted to learn to play again. I had become so focused on work and getting the job done that I neglected the pure delight of play. Actually, it had been this way for a very long time in my life. I've never been all that good at playing. It never seemed to come as naturally to me as working did. When my parents divorced, I must have had to grow up very fast. I took life pretty seriously. Grades took precedence over fun, always. Saturdays were for chores, and Sundays were for church, sometimes. And looking back, church in my early years wasn't all that fun, probably because I didn't have the heart for it. Hobbies were only as good as what they produced, and delight was for the foolish.

I'm not proud of this, but it's the truth.

So when I searched for a sense of wonder and astonishment in my life, I found very little. When I wanted to rediscover delight, I sort of had to start over with discovering it in the first place. Where I saw the delight I was looking for was in the faces of children at play. Children can lose themselves for hours in pure abandonment to delight when they are playing. They are captured and captivated by pretending, imagining, inventing, and creating. I realized I didn't lose myself in anything but work. I held too tightly to everything—my body image, my fears, and my insecurities—to really let go. I began to journal about dreaming, imagining, and creating. I asked God to show me how to delight in play and let me lose myself to it. He began to answer my prayers. I began to listen to my longings and dream new dreams. I started to set aside more time to be creative, and every once in a while I would take myself to the playground for an hour, just to swing.

Relishing Your Senses

Part of the reason I was disconnected from my body was that I was solar systems away from my senses. Intellectually, I knew there were five. Experientially, I couldn't have cared less. I mean, I listened. I kept my eyes open. I enjoyed food. I knew if I touched something hot or if a skunk had died on the road. But my senses were never anything to focus on, let alone relish. After all, aren't they utilitarian? You have them in order to function, right? Hardly. What a world I was missing.

I could never remember the day it happened because this sensual awakening was slow, almost as if my black-and-white life were being colorized one frame at a time. Running began to wake up my body. Being outside, with nothing to do but put one foot in front of the other, was a new experience, and once I got the breathing part down, I had time to look around and notice the leaves on the trees and the color of the sky and the gait of the dog behind the invisible fence. Smells came alive and had names—*honeysuckle* and *car exhaust*. I could feel the breeze on my skin, but more, I noticed it. I could almost taste the wild onions I smelled in the freshly cut grass and the pot roast that had been cooking for hours on a stovetop inside a house. I was finally paying attention.

I can't say it was just the running. Everything in my life at that point was conspiring to wake me up. The counseling in which I was engaged, my creative endeavors in theater, the work on my relationship with my mother, dealing with my anger (this is a big sense-blocker), and journaling were all very significant parts of my awakening. I began to incorporate my senses into every area of my life. I was finally seeing what I had never really seen, feeling my real feelings, enjoying what I enjoyed, and relishing it all. I remember wanting to surround myself with things that looked good, felt good, smelled good, tasted good, and sounded good. Life had become something like a glorious fireworks show. I was more alive than I had ever been in my life.

Luxuriating in the Spirit

Despising your body puts distance between you and the One who created you. I thought I had a good relationship with God, but it was not a passionate one. I was a little too afraid of passion. Passion sounded sexual and dangerous, and I didn't want any part of it. I was too afraid I would just get carried away. But when my spirit opened to my body, my senses, and my new willingness to play, a quickening began to happen in my relationship with God—a dance. God began to reveal himself to me in ways I'd not quite imagined before. It felt as if I had a secret admirer. God was the One who gave me senses to experience and relish; God wanted to be the One to remind me of my worth. I realized that if I would look to him, I could abandon myself and find pure delight in playing. If I was really trusting him to hold my worth and if God really delighted in me as he said he did, I wouldn't have to fear.

God had reached me so deeply through a book called *Life of the Beloved* by Henri Nouwen. Through this amazing work, God called me out of hiding to claim my identity as his loved, adored child. He set my feet on the firmest foundation I'd ever stood upon, and for the first time in my life, I was trusting it to be true.

It was changing everything.

Caught up in new wonder and mystery, I was changing like a caterpillar who simply submits to the transformation thrust upon him by his God-crafted design. I was becoming who God had called me to be. I was waking up and growing up. I was engaging my world as a healing, growing adult, ready to embrace and enjoy all I had been given.

Fresh-Brewed Adventures

- Take a "five senses bath." Light a fragrant candle; put on music. Get a fresh-cut flower, something chocolate or otherwise tasty, and a loofah or mesh sponge, and luxuriate in the tub.
- Stand in front of the mirror every morning for seven days and survey your features. You don't have to have your clothes off, but don't leave until you find one thing you can celebrate about yourself for that day.

I don't really know why, but most people think great sex in marriage is just supposed to happen. If you have chemistry and love, bingo—you're set for life. We've all been to a movie or two—or twenty—that perpetuate this thinking by just telling part of the story. There is more to it. When two flawed, needy, insecure people come together to forge a relationship, it's not always pretty. Relationships don't create our insecurities; they reveal them. *Forge* is a word that means that separate things are brought together in fire to form one new thing. Marriage is a picture of this forging, this melting and molding. Sex plays an important part in making that happen.

Sex is giving the gift of ourselves physically and emotionally to another person. How can we share an honest self with someone else before we are honest with ourselves? Before we have done some work to understand who we are? We can't, which is why so much emphasis remains on the body for sex instead of on the soul, where it belongs. Function has always been less challenging than beauty in the design world. A plumber can make bathtub work, but he can't inspire you to get in it and bathe.

Savoring sexuality as a part of everyday life:

- Be inventive with time
- Create ambience in your space
- Embrace a sexual exploration
- Find new words for communicating
- Give the gift of yourself
- Incorporate play
- Accept permission from God

We barter our personhood for sex when we treat it like something we do rather than an expression of who we are. Women use sex as much as men, but for different reasons. Often women use sex to try to get love, while men use the "talk of love" to try to get sex. But because body and soul are inextricably connected—men and women know inside what they are doing. They settle for taking instead of giving. Worse, this taking is disguised as giving. No wonder it never satisfies. It falls woefully short of how it was designed for us, which in turn creates more shame and more disappointment.

> We can only learn to love by loving.
> —Iris Murdoch

I like the story about a sex support group for intimacy in marriage. Each couple had to reveal how often they were having sex. The answers varied from once a month to three times a week. When one particular couple was about to answer, the man was smiling from ear to ear while the woman seemed a little uncomfortable. The husband was beaming as he told the group, "Once a year." Everyone responded with shock, "Once a year?" Out of the murmurings came the question, "Then how on earth can you be so happy?" With an even bigger smile, he said, "Tonight's the night!"

Directed Journaling

- Write your sexual autobiography.
- Write a sexual mission statement.
- Write out a sexual fantasy.

Throw Another Log on the Fire

One way to continue to encourage your own growth is to pay attention to the couples around you who seem to have vibrant, thriving relationships. (I write *seem* because things are not always as they appear, so you have to study closely.) When a long-married couple seems connected and happy, you can pretty much trust that their sexual relationship is healthy. When you find couples like this, you should be intentional about spending time around them not only to enjoy their company but also to observe the things they do together. You'll discover some of their secrets just by watching them. Here are a few things I've noticed from these kinds of couples:

- They take time for themselves and each other.
- They still send each other cards and give thoughtful gifts.

- They dream together about their future, no matter their age.
- They dance together when the opportunity presents itself.
- They make time for vacations and plan ways to make them special.
- They often volunteer or do some kind of ministry together.

None of these elements are magic bullets that will automatically keep a relationship great because there is very little that is automatic about any relationship. These are just a few of the things I've noticed that couples in healthy relationships do— even inconsistently. They "cut wood" together so they can have a surplus of logs to throw on the fire to keep it going strong, hot, and bright.

Don't give up, dear fresh-brewed reader. Whatever your struggles or issues (and we all have them, so don't give in to feeling alone in this), they are not too big for the God who made you. God will bring healing where you thought there was only brokenness. He will bring comfort where you thought there was only grief. He will bring laughter where you saw anger, and delight in place of angst. Even if your sexual identity as a woman feels strong and your relationship is good, there is always room to grow. We are never finished, and as we gain strength and

> The Eskimo has fifty-two names for snow because it is important to them: there ought to be as many for love."
>
> —Margaret Atwood, Canadian writer

freedom, we are able to help others in the journey toward freedom and hope.

I am much freer today to sit in women's groups and chat about sexuality. I can laugh, and often do, where before I could only sit in silence. I make sure the conversation isn't too superficial and that it stays honest. I always glance around the room to find the sets of eyes that are holding back tears. It is for them that I talk openly about God's hand of healing in my soul and the journey it took to learn (and I'm still learning) to savor and delight in how I was made.

Learning to savor our sexuality doesn't mean we seek to become goddesses, acrobats, lingerie models, or anything that we are not. However, it frees us to embrace or explore such things if we wish to. Savoring means that we are moving toward being open, tender, warm, intimate, inviting, soft, and female. We are moving away from being closed, angry, cold, resentful, hard, and rejecting. Not only toward others, but toward ourselves. We'll pay very close attention to the voice of God calling us his beloved. We'll always want to look better and fresher than we think we do, but we won't let that stop us from being alive and awake. We'll pay attention to our senses, our bodies, and our desires. We'll continue our search for delight and wonder, and study it when we find it. And as often as we can, we'll seek to lose ourselves in play as we offer all that we are, body and soul, to the ones we love.

7

Celebrate Your Friendships

Saturday afternoon at two o'clock. That's what the invitation said. I stared at it daily, my eyes drawn to it like the magnet that held it to our green refrigerator. A birthday party for my friend Andrea. It was an invitation to a new world. I had never been to Andrea's house, and I didn't know if she had any pets or cool games or if she liked the same kind of cake I liked, but the possibilities were endless. Mother and I had already bought a gift for her party, and because it was a cute Barbie outfit, I struggled with a new feeling of having to wait to give someone a gift. Even if it was like every other birthday party—eat too much cake, watch someone open cool presents you wish were yours, run around so long you get a cramp in your side, get your party clothes dirty, and head home worn-out with a surprise piece of candy in your pocket and a big Kool-Aid mustache—it would be wonderful. Birthdays were very important parties when I was little, and they are still important to me today.

A number of years ago, a friend gave me the book *Here and Now* by Henri Nouwen. He put words to what I'd always just felt about these special days: "Birthdays need to be celebrated. I think it is more important to celebrate a birthday than a successful exam, a promotion, or a victory. On a birthday we do not say: 'Thanks for what you did, or said, or accomplished.' No, we say: 'Thank you for being born and being among us.'"

More than just one day a year, the heartbeat of good friendship is this gratitude and joy. Rejoicing, honoring, applauding, commending, saluting, toasting the wonderful people in our lives. Not for what they do, but for who they are and for what they mean to us. Taking the time to say with our words and other expressions, "Thank you for being you." Throwing gratitude parties in our souls.

I didn't discover celebrating my friendships on my own. I first felt what it was like to be celebrated in friendship. I met friends who were able to express this kind of gratitude, and it altered the way I thought about friendship. This cup of fresh-brewed life is dedicated to three wonderful friends: Audrey, Angela, and Denise. Soul mates of the first order, and celebrators extraordinaire. Because friendship, like love, is "caught," not taught, much of what I feel about good friendships I have "caught" from them. It is a pleasure to open a few of my photo albums to you in this chapter and show you some snapshots of friendship celebration.

A word of caution: husbands do not make good girlfriends. How could they? It doesn't even seem fair that we would expect them to care about the fabric we like for the sofa. Okay, maybe they can care about the *one* fabric we like best and are planning to use, and we could release them from touching and feeling the twenty-four hundred we had to eliminate to find the one.

Clearly, that's what girlfriends are for. And while we may know this, it remains tempting to push the men in our lives into a spot reserved for girlfriends. Especially if we are short on girlfriends.

Girlfriends bring out things in us that men simply cannot. Girlfriends understand us differently; they cry with us, shop with us, laugh-till-we-pee with us . . . no man does that! (Nor would we really want one to. Try not to picture it.) Women are sisters who speak the same language, like many of the same movies, often enjoy eating off the same plate, and laugh over the guilt we feel for all the same things.

So what determines friendship? Proximity? Sometimes, but not always. There are women we see every day whom we would no sooner call a friend than fly to the moon. Then there are other women that we have met only one time but wouldn't hesitate to say we've made a friend. What about someone who never lets you down? It sounds good; anyone who has let you down and hurt your feelings wouldn't make a very good friend, right? But most of our closest friends have done that very thing at one time or another. We can all think of people who have never wounded us or disappointed us in any way, but with whom we don't necessarily want to be friends.

> acquaintance, n.: a person whom we know well enough to borrow from, but not well enough to lend to.
> —Ambrose Pierce

Friendships are made over intangible things, qualities that won't be neatly defined or even fully identified. Something inside just clicks. Something in our soul responds. We can't really specify it ahead of time, but we definitely know it when we feel it. In this way, friendship is a mystery. If you ask lifelong friends *why* they are friends, many times they can't even explain it. They can tell you when they met, they can tell you what they do when they are together, but why they are friends? They look at each other and in various ways say something like, "I don't really know. We just are." Then they smile.

With friendship, it's definitely a case of quality over quantity. If you have one close friend, you are blessed and have a good reason to celebrate that relationship. It's important, so nurture it and care for it wisely. If you have two friends, stand up right now and sing the doxology! Wrap your arms around those friends, and praise God, from whom all the blessings of friendship flow. Celebrate each other as often as you can. However, if you are a woman who hasn't found one person in your life to call a close friend and confidante, I'm guessing you're in the ministry! Don't despair; this can change if you want it to. You may just need to make a little space in your life for a "soulish" kind of friend.

> "Stay" is a charming word in a friend's vocabulary.
>
> —Louisa May Alcott

When we meet ourselves coming and going, we don't feel the friendship void; we can't. We can't feel much of anything when we are wall-to-wall committed, least of all how much we may need what feels like one more commitment. How many times have you had a free evening and thought, *Wow, I wish I had one more thing to do or another person to try to get together with?* Never. We think the opposite. *I'm so glad I don't have to go anywhere tonight!* We imagine the possibility of adding on a friendship, and we're thrilled that we haven't. It's hard enough to carve out personal space, let alone cultivate friendship. We wrongly think, *Another friend in my life would just mean more work, and I don't have time for that.*

But then comes the sight of two friends sitting on a bench, conversing deeply, and you may feel a twinge like, *I wish I had a friend like that.* But very quickly you go back to the "I don't have time in my life for one more person" speech. Or you push it from your mind: *I prefer solitude and being by myself,* but inside you know that something is missing.

Others in your life seem to have satisfying friendships. You see women at work or Mother's Day Out, at church or in the grocery store, talking and connecting, and you feel another twinge. But you're firm with your feelings; you don't want to need this. Maybe you're feeling some disappointment in your marriage. Without even knowing it, you've placed unrealistic expectations on your husband to be everything in your life: spouse, lover, friend, God—and you both are stressed because of it. Your children sense some unnameable pressure. *Why is Mom so mad all the time?*

Relax; take a deep breath. The solution is not as hard as you think. You just need a good friend.

You may be saying, "No kidding! I've known for a long time I need a friend, but I can't exactly run to the grocery and pick out someone I can share my soul with." This is true because most of us aren't looking for just any friend. Life is too busy, and we don't carve out time for anything that doesn't impact us. We want soulish friends. A safe place where confidences are held carefully. An oasis of laughter in the middle of our dry lives. But the first step to finding a good friend is to be open to looking for one.

Some women have a group of friends that they have known since grade school. While others, like me, cried out to God for years to bring a close friend. And still others haven't found that person yet. Why do some women have great friendships and others don't? Is it just personality or commitment? How do you find such friends?

Emilie Griffin, in *Clinging*, wrote, "It is hardly a question of finding at all, for nothing we do can ever accomplish it. To 'find' a spiritual friend is truly to be found, to be chased down, smoked out of one's hiding place in the corner of existence."

So stay open; we look, and we wait to be found. No one likes waiting, so I suggest celebrating in the meantime. Even if your friendships aren't exactly what you're looking for, celebrating can turn the wait into an adventure. Who knows what may happen.

Throwing a Party

Celebrating your friendships looks just like throwing a party; the elements are the same. Here are five simple things you need in order to celebrate your friendships:

1. An Invitation—Time

Getting an invitation to anything is a special occasion. Whether it comes in a phone call, a letter, an e-mail, or smoke signals, the message is, "Your presence is requested." The excitement is undeniable. An invitation piques our curiosity and starts us imagining wonderful things. It doesn't really matter if it's Cinderella at the ball, a dinner at the White House, or Tuesday morning coffee with your neighbor. We love being invited. Even if we can't attend, it feels good to have been invited. Inviting is active. Inviting says, "I was thinking about you, and I am requesting your presence." Inviting says, "I have made time for you and me to celebrate." Inviting makes a hopeful promise of good times.

> Good communication is as stimulating as black coffee, and just as hard to sleep after.
>
> —Anne Morrow Lindbergh

Angela and I had been casual friends for several years, but we had never spent much time together. Then came this invitation. "I am going to a Christmas benefit, and I would love to have you go with me. I would like to get to know you better."

I look for reasons to make invitations. Occasionally I wake up and think, *Who can I invite today, and for what?* It's almost like a dare. I'm thinking of designing personal stationery that simply says, "Your presence is requested." Then I can use it for every-thing: birthdays, holidays, Wednesdays, *Seinfeld* reruns, pouring concrete, you name it—come over.

An inviting home also makes a hopeful promise of good times. The minute anyone walks in the front door of Audrey's house, it calls out, saying, "You are welcome here; stay and spend time." Her home is merely a reflection of her heart. Can we have any higher calling than to invite our friends to that place? To say to them, "You are welcome here in my life; stay and spend time." What an invitation!

2. A Gift—Yourself

Denise looked at the clock. It was two in the morning. We'd been sitting for five hours on my sofa, completely engrossed in conversation. The flame on the gas logs was dancing, the house was silent, and we were just getting started. We were going deep. We don't get together enough to have the luxury of superficiality.

To the party of friendship, you must bring a gift. You've been invited, remember? "Your presence is requested." *My presence?* It would be far easier to bring a kitchen gadget. C. S. Lewis cautions us that we may act kindly, correctly, justly . . . and yet withhold the giving of ourselves, which is love. To offer a vulnerable nug-get of your soul that has been mined from a deep, sometimes dark, place is more valuable than gold to your friend, and she will receive it as a great gift.

3. Confetti—Encouragement

I love throwing things up in the air. Isn't it fun? At weddings or on New Year's Eve, everybody wants something in their hands to throw. It's a unique way of lavishing or throwing our love on people. Confetti becomes a tangible expression of intangible emotions. It's happy, fun, and free.

Taking the time to gather little pieces of love, grace, strength, and hope is worth it when you can shower your friendships with them. Encouragement is spiritual confetti!

Over many years, Angela has celebrated our friendship with this kind of confetti. She has left amazing voice mails for me when I am discouraged. She also sends me e-mails and texts, like this one: "Just wanted you to know I am praying for you. I will always stand in the gap for you, for our friendship, and for our ministries. You are a treasure, my sister. I love you. Press on, Angela."

When we are together, she prays for me and with me, building me up by her words and example. We have shared so much of our journey together, and the value of our friendship is great cause for celebration.

Encouragement is to a friendship what confetti is to a party. It's light, refreshing, and fun, and you always end up finding little pieces of it stuck on you later.

4. A Great Cake—A Good Plan and Lots of Laughter

A good friend was having party, and I was bringing the cake. I didn't want just any cake. I wanted something that would hurt when you ate it. A cake so good you wish you could dive into it in your swimsuit. You get the idea, something stellar. When I called the bakery a friend recommended as "the one," I was told I should have placed an order two days ahead of time! I was used to walking into the grocery and picking up a cake. For something really special, for a real celebration, sometimes you just have to plan.

This goes against the sanguine personality who likes to let things happen as they will. Most of the time that's fine, as celebrations should be spontaneous. But every once in a while, make a plan. Call and schedule the trip, book the tennis court, put together an amazing day. It will communicate loud and clear that you thought about this ahead of time and took extra care to make it special.

Audrey celebrates our friendship by planning. When I arrive at her home, I am usually exhausted. She knows I am too tired to make decisions, so she takes care of every last one. I just want to spend time with her and give her all the energy I have. And I have a lot more energy when I don't have to decide where to eat, what to eat, or which movie to see.

To me, laughing with friends is as good as eating cake at a party. You can have a party without cake, but who would want to? Every close friend I have loves to laugh and doesn't take herself, or me, too seriously. Laughter is like a tall, creamy, beautiful, four-layered cake that kinda leans to one side. A cake like that is meant to be cut and shared. Forks all around and enjoyment beyond belief. It feels great to lose yourself in laughter. Doubled over, knees pressed together so you don't pee, face red, tears rolling down your cheeks. Trying to regain composure, acting overly serious, only to lose it all over again.

5. The Cleanup—Shared Burdens

Part of celebrating is cleaning up. Burdens are something that we share in friendship. I find this very difficult sometimes, just like letting friends help with the dishes. I know I need a little help, but it feels bad to ask. In the party of life, real friends are the ones who hang around to help you do the dishes, literally and figuratively. They aren't the ones who ask if they can help—they're the ones who just get busy.

My closest friends have all done my dishes at one time or another. They have carried my burdens on so many occasions. I have to let them into the messy kitchen of my life and humbly ask for a little help. It shouldn't be so hard to do this, but it always is. Each friend, in her own way, rolls up her sleeves and gets to work. They never try to fix me or fix things for me; they just stand by my side with their hands in the same dirty water. They

> It's the friends you can call at four in the morning that really matter.
>
> —Marlene Dietrich

aren't afraid of my mess, even when I am afraid to show it to them. Their presence reminds me they are in my life to celebrate our friendship, from the first invitation through the last dish.

Do a quick inventory of the friends you've invited into your life. Of those with whom you spend time, do you have one or more about whom you could say these things?

- "We share our lives, and make time for each other."
- "We hold each other's personal issues in confidence."
- "I could call or have called this person at four in the morning."
- "If my marriage were in trouble, I could talk to her about it openly."
- "We'll be friends in twenty years."

Like a Lovely Bouquet

Looking for reasons to celebrate, I uncover gratitude. I realize how much I have to be thankful for. Spending time with my friends allows me to stay in that place of gratitude a little while longer. Celebrating birthdays, victories, answered prayers, and accomplishments allows me to acknowledge them before I have to move on to something else. Throwing "a party," even if it's just a cup of coffee shared together to mark a worthy moment, is great for the soul.

I mentioned previously in this chapter that I've learned about celebrating from the best: Audrey has come to the airport for a short visit between my connecting flights. Denise has rearranged her busy corporate workday on several occasions to run a critical errand for me. Once, Angela drove a couple hours just to meet me for breakfast when I was in a not-so-nearby city. Obviously, I've never forgotten these celebrations. I have been by myself, five hundred miles from the closest of them, and

Fresh-Brewed Adventures

- Celebrate your spiritual birthday, or someone else's. Make a picnic lunch, have a party, or just enjoy a piece of cake in honor of your rebirth into the family of God. Celebrate being found by him!
- Request the honor of someone's presence. Practice inviting. Invite your daughter to join you on an errand that you normally do by yourself. Write an invitation to a friend to meet you for a cup of coffee or tea or lemonade and bring along a book for her, just because. Invite someone to attend church or a Bible study with you and bring killer cookies.
- Plan an extravagant, expensive, special day with a close friend. Think of as many fun things as possible to squeeze into one day. Give your friend a copy of the expensive day you planned; then do something inexpensive and spontaneous together.
- Pay attention to your dog. Dogs really know how to celebrate. Pick up some helpful suggestions from their behavior: hang your head out the window, wag your tail when you see people you love, enjoy your food, nap anywhere.

something one of these friends has said or done will cause me to smile or even laugh out loud. I have exponentially more joy in my life because of them. Friendship fills a deep well within me with fresh, clean water. When I celebrate my friendships, it's like dropping a huge rock into the well. It splashes that water everywhere, on everyone else in my life.

Like a Swarm of Bees

Annie Dillard wrote about a young friend with whom she gets together a few times a year: "Now she is aware of some of the losses you incur by being here—the extortionary rent you have to pay as long as you stay. We have lived together so often, and parted so many times, that the very sight of each other means loss. The ever-taller embrace of our hellos is a tearful affair, aware as we are of our imminent parting; fortunately the same anticipation cancels our goodbyes, and we embrace cheerfully, like long-lost kin at a reunion."

In her wonderful writing style and choice of words, Annie explained something I've long felt when seeing my long-distance friends. "The very sight of each other means loss." There is so much excitement before a visit, and it seems I'm not there long before the heaviness sets in. We will have to part soon, and each of us will be alone again. The longing sets in—I want to live in a world where there is no parting. I know I have issues about separating from those I love that probably come from parting with my father for so many years, but when I feel it sometimes, it just seems too high a cost. Maybe I should try to form a better friendship with the eighty-year-old man next door!

I have a friend.
I sing louder.
I smile bigger.
I laugh harder.
I pray more.
I love better.

Audrey and her husband, Randy, are avid gardeners or, as I call them, *botanical artists*—not by profession but by love. In their backyard they have created a little secret garden. I wrote a good bit of the longings chapter in that wonderful spot, as I tucked myself away amid the flowers and stones. One particular morning I was listening to the fountain, cherishing the simple beauty surrounding me. I was relishing my senses fully. During a break, I complimented Audrey on her work, the loveliness that I was appreciating and enjoying as I wrote. Audrey told me a story about one of her friends who doesn't care for wasps and bees. (As if some people do?) As a result, this friend won't plant flowers in her backyard because she doesn't want the bees. From amid the beauty that surrounded me, I decided that's a pretty high price. I relate that to the high cost of a long-distance relationship. There are many challenges for sure, but for me the beauty they bring far outweighs the bees.

Directed Journaling

- Make a list of special people in your life, from your spouse all the way to the lady at the dry cleaners. Think of ways to celebrate their presence in your life—a thank-you, a smile, a special card. As you write their names in your journal, say a special prayer for each one.
- Ask yourself, "Am I too busy for meaningful friendship?" and be honest about your answer.
- What are some of the dishes (problems in your life) that you need to let your friends help you with?
- Celebrate your friendship with God today. Write some words to him telling him what his friendship means to you.

Keep the Celebration Going

Enjoying this cup of fresh-brewed life is not intended to call you to form an exclusive circle of friends. The goal is to celebrate life by celebrating your friends. A celebrating that helps us become more loving, more caring, and more gracious, creating a ripple effect that will touch every area of our lives.

Celebrate your family. "We're not friends; we're family!" Whether that is true for you or not, our families are always in need of celebration. Throwing a party, figuratively, can make struggling relationships good and good relationships better. Celebrating says to our families that they matter and they are important in our lives. They are the easiest to take for granted because they're family and because of scheduled celebrations, like holidays and birthdays. We know we are going to see them eventually, so we think we don't have to be proactive about getting together. Setting up something intentionally can make a great statement.

Celebrate your friendship with God. God, through Christ, has become our friend. Exodus 33:11 says: "The LORD would speak to Moses face to face, as a man speaks with his friend." As you are journaling in the mornings, celebrate your friendship with God. Invite him to speak to you, bring yourself to him as a gift, give him praise, laugh, and share your burdens. Make it a little party. Allow your relationship with him to deepen to a new level of intimacy. Your friendship with God is not a stepping-stone to a "real" relationship; it is the cornerstone of all relationships.

> Selfishness is not living as one wishes to live, it is asking others to live as one wishes to live.
>
> —Ruth Rendell

You can set the table perfectly, buy a beautiful dessert, open a fantastic bottle of wine, and still not celebrate. Celebration comes from the heart. It is gratitude doing the tango. It is a jack-in-the-box of joy. It is unabashed exultation in the delight of connecting with a friend. Better fried chicken in the company of your closest companions than chateaubriand in the mansion of an enemy. Real celebration cannot be manufactured, nor would you ever want it to be. It is authentic, spontaneous, and deeply spiritual. It is a smile that begins in your soul. Give yourself permission to celebrate your friendships. Let go. Make a big deal over them. Go ahead and fuss a little. You can always go back to humdrum tomorrow. Humdrum doesn't go anywhere; it will still be there in the morning. Today, make the most of your fresh-brewed life, and celebrate.

8

Change Your World

Karen finally got the kids down for the night. Someone had called in the middle of the nighttime routine, and not being free to check, she'd let it go to voice mail. Turned out it was her mother, with the sad news that Dad was back in the hospital. She was trying to fix something for dinner for Rick, who was working late for the overtime pay, with Christmas right around the corner. She microwaved some leftover pasta, thinking about the shopping she still had left to do and wondering how she could rearrange her day tomorrow to go see her father. She'd gotten two boxes of decorations down from the attic and was on her way up for a third when a text message from her dentist's office reminded her of an appointment she'd completely forgotten. Her life felt like one endless string of interruptions as long as the lights she still needed to put on the naked tree in the corner. Everywhere Karen looked, things were half-done. Groceries still on the counter, half put away; schedule now up in the air for tomorrow; half-eaten dinner plates on the table from the kids; and cold air coming down from the pull-down to the attic, where half of the Christmas decorations still waited for her. She thought to herself, *I don't have a life—just half of a life. Why can't I finish one thing?*

She tried to kick her spirit into high gear. Rick would be home soon, and if she could get the dishes done, the groceries put away, and something on the table for him, it would look as though she had accomplished something, even if didn't feel that way. She could never give an account of where all her time went. She knew she'd done all she could, but it never seemed like enough; there was always more that didn't get done. The laundry was in piles, half-finished, and there were at least two people she was supposed to call today, but for the life of her she couldn't remember who they were or why. She felt a familiar panic. On the brink of rushing headlong into "frenzy mode," she stopped herself and took a deep breath.

With that breath, Karen—daughter, mother, wife—did something she'd never had the emotional strength to do before. She put water on for a cup of tea, just for herself. She took another deep breath and contemplated her choice of Ginger Peach or Lemon Mint. She turned on some Christmas music, stacked some dishes in the sink for later, and put away just the perishable things from the grocery bags. She sat down with her Bible in the middle of the Christmas decorations and read Luke 2. "O Come, All Ye Faithful" was gently soothing her ruffled spirit. She prayed and asked God to bring peace amid the chaos. She had no idea that what she had taken time to do would change her whole world.

Some of us "get 'er done," type A women try so hard to make a difference in our world that we actually undo the difference we hope to make by our damaging striving. We have exchanged changing the world for running the world; there is a painful difference. Changing the world involves intentional action and trust, while running the world involves control and fear. I don't think I have to name names here; we know who we are, right?

Women have a deep desire to create purpose and meaning in their lives. This is a given. It's how we are made. I haven't met one woman yet who said, "I want to look back on my life and realize that it didn't count for anything!" I don't know if men realize this about women. Some men think when it comes to words like significance or legacy, they are the only ones who want to make it count. As if doing "man's work" is the only way, or even the best way to leave a mark on this world. In that thinking is the implication that changing diapers every day or trying to get peas into the mouth of a moving target isn't significant work! I'm sad to say that women have bought into this thinking as well. *I don't get paid for what I do, so what my husband does is somehow more important.* More important for paying the bills, yes, but for changing the world? Not so sure about that one. It's not a competition, but I don't think any man would appreciate his boss coming into his office about four thirty, looking at his desk, and saying, "Look at this mess! What have you been doing all day?"

Women who work outside their homes also want to make a difference, but when asked something like, "Do you want to change the world?" many reply, "How on earth could I do that?" Women are intimidated by the question; we think changing the world is too big for us. That's better left to someone more talented or articulate. *How could I change the world? There is nothing remarkable in what I do. I raise kids. I drive the car pool. I'm not going to invent anything or influence anyone. I don't wear makeup to the grocery store. I can't even find my car keys. Change the world? You've got to be kidding!* But inside, we have a deep need to know that what we are doing matters.

Creating a fresh-brewed life steaming with significance doesn't just happen. Our actions and activities have to be intentional. Order doesn't magically arise out of chaos. It must be created and then maintained. Often the small semblances of order we sometimes achieve degenerate into chaos in no time. If we simply let our days run their course, we will not find order or meaning. We will find ourselves stuck.

One day a husband was in the kitchen with his wife while she prepared a ham for baking. She started by cutting both ends off the ham, something he'd seen her do many times.

"Honey, why do you cut the ends off?" Expecting a reason that warranted such wasting, he was surprised when she answered, "Because that's the way my mother always prepped a ham."

Now they both wanted a better answer. The woman called her mother to ask why she cut the ends off the ham every time she cooked one. Her mother confessed, "I'm not really sure; it's just the way my mother did it when I was growing up. It must have had something to do with their health back then."

Had her grandmother been alive, the woman would have called to settle the question, but she left it and soon forgot about it. Several weeks later she was at a party with her aunt. She recounted the conversations from the ham question that her husband had first posed. The woman's aunt began laughing immediately. "You know, I asked her that once, when I was in the kitchen with her." The aunt was still smiling as she said, "Mom laughed and said it was the only way she could make it fit in the pan!"

Are you doing things others have done, just because you never thought about doing things differently? Are you cutting out pieces of your life for no good reason? We have more pans than our grandmothers did. We have opportunities and choices they never had or even dreamed of. I'm not saying you can have it all (you can't) or that you won't find yourself needing to trim some parts (you will), but don't get stuck thinking you can't build the life you want because you've never done it that way before. Loosen up your creativity to find a few different pans!

Open up your spirit to the possibility that you can be an agent of change in your world.

Let's explore this cup of fresh-brewed life in five different sips.

1. Face Your Fear

Have you ever found yourself thinking, *What I do doesn't really matter. Nobody lives or dies based on how many loads of laundry I do today.* (Well, maybe your husband's coworkers do.) *What difference does it make if I show up for work or not?* We think our contribution to life isn't very significant. *All I do is clean up after people and cook meals.* Or maybe you think, *I just work at a nine-to-five job. I don't make much money. I'm not in the ministry, and I don't see myself becoming a missionary.* We have come to accept that having little meaning, passion, or purpose in our lives is normal. The sad truth is, it probably is. But living the way everyone else lives doesn't mean it is how we were made to live.

Some women don't want others to notice their accomplishments. They downplay everything. They worry that if they are good at what they do, other women might think things like: *She is just trying to get attention. She really wants power and prestige; that's not godly.* So they shrink, never daring to attempt great things. Out of fear, they miss what God is calling them to do or, worse, refuse to do it for reasons of plain old fear. And that's not godly.

In fact, in the parable of the talents (Matt. 25:14–30), Jesus tells a story of three people who were given different amounts of money to use and multiply. The master gave one man five talents, another man two talents, and another just one. When the master returned later, he asked what each had done with what he had been given. The first two had multiplied their talents in different ways and showed the master something they had done with what he had given them. The last fellow confessed that he had hidden all his money away because he was afraid.

I've heard sermons on this parable about making the most of what you've been given. You could definitely look at it that way. But to me, this story is a picture of fear in action—or better, inaction. Many women have dreams of writing books, starting companies, staying home from work with their children, or getting more involved with a particular ministry, but they fail to act because of fear.

Remember from the Listen to Your Longings chapter that fear of disappointment usually pushes us in one of two directions? We either become spectators, watching, or we become evaluators, criticizing. *Why would I write a book? My friend is the author, not me. I have something to say, but I don't think anyone would care.* Or what about, *What's the big deal about writing poetry? I could write that—anyone could.*

Neither position moves us toward action, both lead to inaction when we let fear win. Nothing gets written, and God (who doesn't need you to write or not write) is sad because you are afraid when you don't have to be.

Nothing fails like success because we don't learn from it. We only learn from failure.

—Kenneth Boulding

In this parable, the story doesn't imply that the first two men did everything right to multiply what they had been given. It basically says that they just did *something*. They made a difference because they opened their hands and used what they had been given.

Are you tightly clutching what you have? Afraid to let the world see the gifts God has given you because the world might not embrace them or understand them? Maybe the fear of failing—or the fear of succeeding—has you burying your talent and doing nothing.

I have had the privilege of hearing Tim Keller speak on many occasions. Tim is the founding pastor of Redeemer Presbyterian

Church in New York City. I've never been to his church, but he has been a shepherd to my mind and heart for decades through his messages and books. During a very memorable conference session together, he asked this question: "Did you buy into Christianity to serve God or to have God serve you?"

We serve God when we face our fear and use what he has given us and how he has designed us to change the world around us. He's given us all we need. God doesn't call us to change the world only to worry that we can't really do it—he supplies all that we need, and more, to do what he's called us to do. We need not fear anymore. We can rest in this. We can rest in him.

2. Get Control of Your Schedule

Have you ever thought about what you might want written on your tombstone? This can seem like a morbid thought, so we don't go there much, but it happens to be an important question—one that is far more helpful to us in life than in death. If you could stand around at your own funeral and hear people talk about what they remember about you, what would you want them to be saying?

The tombstone doesn't ask, "What did you do in your life?" It asks, "What did you do *with* your life?" This deeper question gets to the core of what we really value in life and is just as important for a stay-at-home mom to answer as it is for the president of a Fortune 500 company.

An epitaph is very big-picture. It seeks to capture the most important aspect of your life, heart, and soul. The words are etched after your death, so they are typically written by someone else—someone looking at your life from the outside. Surveying what you "did" and how you spent your time. Do your heart and soul come out in what you do? People may look at your calendar of activities and completely miss what you would want them to see.

When we are honest, most of our days are full of things that we don't want to be doing. It is hard to find epitaph material in those activities. What woman in her right mind would want "This Woman Could Iron" carved in stone above her head? If the deepest, most prominent desire of her heart is to be a loving, caring mother, she may need to unplug the iron a little more often and get on the floor and play. Making ham sandwiches can be a means to the end you seek if done with great love. But mothers can also get lost in the bread and mayo and miss the real meat. When our schedules have control of our time, we must ask if they also have control of our hearts. When this is true, our real focus is on the tasks, not on the kids. It is our job to make sure the majority of our schedule reflects the majority of our heart to the best of our abilities.

Time can be our enemy when it comes to changing our world. Little things we never have time to do can often yield the most profound results: a conversation with your neighbor, a Yahtzee game with your teenager, taking food to a sick friend's family, reading with your child. When we let our schedules get the best of us, we cannot have the kind of impact we really long for because we can't pause to make a difference. We are too focused on getting it done, on finishing. I confess in my brokenness that there have been times I've loved my "to do" list more than the ones I'm trying "to do" it for. For what? For the sake of getting it all done? We will never get it all done. Ever. It's a setup, a trap. There will always be more to do—more ironing, more cleaning, more phone calls, more business travel, you name it. But special moments with your children, significant dates with your family, opportunities to help someone in need, these require us to press PAUSE or STOP. If for no other reason than to remind ourselves that we are in control of our schedules, and it's not the other way around.

I really appreciate this quote from Lee Iacocca, former head of Chrysler: "I'm constantly amazed by the number of people who can't seem to control their own schedules. Over the years, I've had many executives come to me and say with pride, 'Boy, last year I worked so hard that I didn't take any vacation.' It's actually nothing to be proud of. I always feel like responding, 'You dummy. You mean to tell me that you can take responsibility for an $80 million project, and you can't plan two weeks out of the year to go off with your family and have some fun?'"

Controlling your schedule doesn't necessarily mean that you have to be home a certain number of hours or must schedule large chunks of time with nothing to do. While both could be good, neither will necessarily help you change your world. Plenty of people have time to pay attention, but don't. Controlling your schedule means your life reflects your priorities. If you feel as I do that God has put us here for more than paying our bills or playing the Wii, then don't let busyness rob you of your impact. Keeping a rein on your calendar will help to make this a reality. Our hearts *and* calendars must be available to God.

3. Find Your Passion

What does it profit a woman to gain the whole world if she loses her own soul? Or in my language, "Do I win if I complete all the tasks but lose my sanity in the process?" What would it profit a woman to get all the laundry done but miss living the life God had for her?

I am a recovering Superwoman. I put my résumé in three times but never got the job. Probably because of those dang tights. I do have God-given gifts, but more often, I just have a hard time saying no. Not so proud of this. Nothing robs my life of meaning or purpose faster than simply saying yes to something that my heart is not in. The amount of work we take on doesn't necessarily correspond with the impact we have. Burnout, crabbiness, resentment, lack of gratitude—these are the gifts of the overachievers. Not so blessed, are they? These are the rotten fruits of the spirit! Conversely, they come from doing too much, out from under the power or control (or grace) of God. We can't change the world by taking on the world. Remember, there is a difference between changing your world and trying to run the world. Namely, enjoyment and satisfaction versus resentment and exhaustion.

> From most of history, Anonymous was a woman.
> —Virginia Woolf

Between supper, baths, and bedtime, or meetings, phone calls, and commuting, what woman has time to think about creating meaning? Doesn't that sound like taking on something else? Susan Douglas wrote in *Where the Girls Are*, "Study after study shows that while working dads have time to read the paper, to watch guys with arms the size of Smithfield hams run into each other, to go out with boys for a frosty one, or simply to take a nap, working moms barely have time—or the opportunity—to pee with the bathroom door fully closed." Even if her examples are no longer exactly true in our "Helpful Dad" culture, it sure does feel this way at times.

If we don't feel we can pee with the door closed, how in the heck are we going to change the world? Take a deep breath. Pursuing significance or seeking to change your world doesn't necessarily mean taking on anything new. It might mean doing an analysis of your gifts and getting control of your schedule and then listening to God for directions. Go back to that epitaph I asked you about. How do you want to be remembered? What motivates you to work? This passion that we are looking for is not the *what* so much as it is the *why*. What gets you out of bed in the morning? Please don't say your alarm clock; I can't bear it. Is there something God is calling you to? Sit with your journal out, and just listen. Then write down what he tells you.

I have heard a friend say, "The deepest question of our lives is not 'If you died tonight, do you know where you would spend eternity?' That's a good question, and one that must be settled, but the deeper question is 'If you wake up tomorrow, do you know how you will spend the rest of your life?'" As Christians, a lot of us aren't afraid of dying. We're more afraid of living. Especially if we don't know what we are living for. If we have a relationship with Christ, we believe he will be there for us when we die, but what kind of life is he calling us to live?

I don't think the knowledge of what our passion is gets handed to us like a gift. More likely, it is revealed in us and to us over time, like the way a sculptor creates a work. Everything extra gets chiseled away. Sometimes we can glimpse our passion by identifying all the things we know it's not. While that doesn't always reveal it, it can bring about new clarity. Author Bob Buford wrote about this "one thing" that we are seeking to discover in his best-selling book *Half Time*. "All I can tell you with any degree of certainty is that you will not find an abiding sense of purpose and direction by rushing from business appointment to church meeting to your son's soccer game to dinner with friends and then to bed. If you cannot afford to take the time and solitude before God that finding your 'one thing' requires, you are not ready to find it."

> We can do no great things—only small things with great love.
>
> —Mother Teresa

Finding your passion is critical for changing your world. If for no other reason than it will save you energy and bring you joy. It isn't "one more thing" to add to your plate—it is the plate itself. When we work out of our God-given passion, we get tired but not weary. We still need rest but not a change. Uncovering God's purpose in your life and following it will lead you to greater satisfaction in your work and much more abundant living.

Many women don't think they need a passion in life—just

work. When you meet one of these women, if feels as though she has defined serving God as the hardest, worst thing she could think of to do, but she is called, and she will finish the work even though she complains about it the whole time. There is no joy in such women's lives, no "change-the-world spirit," just an angry expectation of brownie points in heaven for having taken the hard road while others wimped out by doing something they enjoy. This kind of life is as stale as two-day-old coffee and just as appealing.

Directed Journaling

- Make a list of phrases that you would love to hear people say about you at your funeral.
- Start thinking about what you would be honored to have written on your tombstone.
- What, if any, gifts has God given you that you aren't using for him?
- What is your passion, that "one thing" you want your life to be about?

4. Stop Waiting for Your Life to Begin

Say this out loud (if you're alone in the room): "The quality of my life is determined by one thing: my attitude toward it." Now say it again.

Our quality of life is not determined by our circumstances, but we can let it be. It isn't determined by our health, but we can believe it to be. It isn't determined by our bank accounts, but we can choose it to be. No, the one thing that truly determines the quality of the life we have is the attitude that we bring to it.

There was a businessman I knew. I'll call him Frank. Frank was looking to hire an assistant. I suggested he call another friend of mine whom he respected to see if she might have a recommendation for him. So Frank called my friend Judy and said he was looking for another employee. Before Judy had the chance to feel honored, he said, "I want someone just like you. Someone who isn't out to change the world; she just wants to do her job." Judy was crushed. So much so that she didn't want to tell me that Frank had even called. Later, when I asked her about it, she couldn't stop the tears. She was so hurt, and understandably so. If you knew Judy, you would know she is out to change the world—the world of the person she is working for. By her competent and professional skills and her positive attitude, she is changing the world. Ironically, that's what Frank liked about Judy, yet he lacked the eyes to see it or the heart to appreciate it.

You don't have to change jobs to find meaning and purpose, but you may have to change your perspective. You don't have to wait until your kids go to school or you are free to volunteer; you can start today. Find the meaning in today. Don't miss the life that is in front of you; mine it for the meaning that is there—and make intentional choices to make the work that you're doing about something deeper than the work itself. It is the means to the end that you're aiming for.

Sarah Ban Breathnach wrote in *Simple Abundance*, "If I do not endow my life and my work with meaning, no one will ever be able to do it for me." If you don't think enough meaning exists in your life, create it in the midst. Don't just run errands; use the opportunity to meditate. Pray for the businesses in your community that you have to visit. Your bank and your dry cleaners both could use your prayers. God has created you for a life of meaning and purpose. Enjoy it. Don't just gulp down a quick bite; choose to "dine" on peanut butter and jelly. Take it outside somewhere, chew it slowly (I promise this won't set your day back by much), savor the taste of it, enjoy the moment to breathe, and see the beauty. If you don't think you see beauty, keep looking until you can recognize and be grateful for one beautiful thing. Celebrate the significance and wonder of life in the present moment. Is it just a quick lunch break for energy, or is it an opportunity?

Look for the extraordinary in the ordinary. In your short or long drive to work tomorrow, try to notice a few things you pass every day and never pay attention to. Perhaps you'll see someone crying in the car next to you, the sunrise that rarely registers, the new shrubs in the neighbor's yard. The possibilities are endless. You may notice an opportunity to help someone in need, have a great idea for a new business, or see something that makes you want to call your dad. Things of meaning and beauty that have been there all along, waiting for you to see, but missed due to being in your own world, while paying half attention to the real one.

> **Character cannot be developed in ease and quiet. Only through experience of trial and suffering can the soul be strengthened, vision cleared, ambition inspired, and success achieved.**
>
> —Helen Keller

One morning while traveling, I ducked into a little diner to get a cup of coffee and a bagel. I commented to the waitress as I was leaving, "Hope you have a good day."

"How can it be good when I'm working?" she asked, laughing.

I was almost out the door, but I stopped and went back in a little ways. "Don't postpone your life until you get off work." She smiled and then laughed again. I hoped she would take my advice. The quality of her day would be determined by her attitude toward it.

Can you have a good day if you have to work? Can you allow yourself to enjoy even the most mundane tasks simply because it is the work that has been given you for the day? I'm not talking about getting it done; I'm talking about enjoying it. If so, you are living a fresh-brewed life, and you can't help but change the world. It will be changed by your presence—by your freedom to live above your circumstances and responsibilities.

To close this section, I'm including a piece I came across. It speaks to this issue of not postponing our lives. It speaks not to changing our circumstances but rather our perspective on them. It touched me deeply.

A Story to Live By
by Ann Wells (*Los Angeles Times*)

My brother-in-law opened the bottom drawer of my sister's bureau and lifted out a tissue-wrapped package. "This," he said, "is not a slip. This is lingerie." He discarded the tissue and handed me the slip. It was exquisite; silk, handmade and trimmed with a cobweb of lace. The price tag with an astronomical figure on it was still attached. "Jan bought this the first time we went to New York, at least 8 or 9 years ago. She never wore it. She was saving it for a special occasion. Well, I guess this is the occasion." He took the slip from me and put it on the bed with the other clothes we were taking to the mortician. His hands lingered on the soft material for a moment, then he slammed the drawer shut and turned to me. "Don't ever save anything for a special occasion. Every day you're alive is a special occasion."

I remembered those words through the funeral and the days that followed when I helped him and my niece attend to all the sad chores that follow an unexpected death. I thought about them on the plane returning to California from the Midwestern town where my sister's family lives. I thought about all the things that she had done without realizing that they were special.

I'm still thinking about his words, and they've changed my life. I'm reading more and dusting less. I'm sitting on the deck and admiring the view without fussing about the weeds in the garden.

I'm spending more time with my family and friends and less time in committee meetings. Whenever possible, life should be a pattern of experience to savor, not endure. I'm trying to recognize these moments now and cherish them.

I'm not "saving" anything; we use our good china and crystal for every special event—such as losing a pound, getting the sink unstopped, the first camellia blossom.

I wear my good blazer to the market if I feel like it. My theory is if I look prosperous, I can shell out $28.49 for one small bag of groceries without wincing. I'm not saving my good perfume for special parties; clerks in hardware stores and tellers in banks have noses that function as well as my party-going friends'.

"Someday" and "one of these days" are losing their grip on my vocabulary. If it's worth seeing or hearing or doing, I want to see and hear and do it now. I'm not sure what my sister would have done had she known that she wouldn't be here for the tomorrow we all take for granted. I think she would have called my family members and a few close friends. She might have called a few former friends to apologize and mend fences for past squabbles. I like to think she would have gone out for a Chinese dinner, her favorite food. I'm guessing—I'll never know.

It's those little things left undone that would make me angry if I knew that my hours were limited. Angry because I put off seeing good friends whom I was going to get in touch with—someday. Angry because I hadn't written certain letters that I intended to write—one of these days. Angry and sorry that I didn't tell my husband and daughter often enough how much I truly love them. I'm trying very hard not to put off, hold back, or save anything that would add laughter and luster to our lives.

And every morning when I open my eyes, I tell myself that it is special.

Every day, every minute, every breath truly is . . . a gift from God.

Fresh-Brewed Adventures

- Get out your good china tonight, even if you're going to eat in front of the television.
- Wear your favorite blazer, spray your best perfume, and head out just to run errands.
- Decide one special thing you can do at work that gives your job more meaning.

5. Learn to Receive Praise

Why are we so afraid of accepting kind words? We deflect them and let them bounce off us rather than take them in. We must think it's more spiritual to do this. However, when we receive words of criticism, we take them right to our core. Do we really believe it is more holy to let critical words into our soul while authentic praise or encouragement stands outside in the cold?

A number of years ago, a friend taught me a good lesson about receiving praise. She handed me a little stack of letters that I'd finished reading and put in the trash. "Why are you throwing these away?" Cindy asked.

"Why would I keep them?" I replied, embarrassed. *What do you do with a letter telling you how wonderful you are after you've already read it?* "It feels a little self-centered."

"I'll keep them for you," she answered. "You may want them one day."

That day, Cindy began my first "Applause" file.

It's a helpful tool because I don't always know what to do with praise. Having a file helps me put it somewhere. I'm not discarding it; I'm keeping it. It's a way of thanking God for the work he's done—and the praise I've received because of it. Even though it belongs to him, people have given it to me, so I'll hold it for him. Sometimes at the end of the day, or the month, or the year, I'll read those notes or cards, giving them to him in gratitude for the work he's given me (and gifted me) to do for him.

Spiritual anorexia is a condition that causes us to refuse the things, like praise, that will nourish our souls. Just like the physical manifestation, spiritually it is a control issue as well. Women are starving for affirmation, encouragement, and praise. We are thirsty for someone to think we are doing a good job at something, anything. Yet we turn down praise because we think it will make us appear arrogant if we accept it. I think it's the other way around. I sense far more arrogance in people who continually deflect compliments or applause. They go to great lengths to point out it's not them or they point up to God—that it's him. As an audience member, I feel I can't offer my praise without being chided about a better way to offer it; therefore, they cannot accept it.

Say thank you, and take it. Don't deflect it and act as though it were nothing. Don't try to pass the glory straight to God . . . just receive it as it is offered. Don't dismiss it or trivialize it or wave it away. Accept it. Take it into your soul, and allow it to nourish you. Then later, prayerfully, thankfully, and humbly (in secret, when it counts) acknowledge your Creator. Give him the praise that was given to you. Hand him the glory that someone handed to you. Keep the card in a special place or write the words you were given in your journal. Next time you are feeling discouraged, go to that place and allow God to remind you that he is using you to change your world.

Living a fresh-brewed life will change your world. As you offer your talents to God, he will mulitiply them. When you get control of your schedule, his fingerprints will show up all over your life. And when you discover and embrace the passion that God has created in you, the warmth that you have to share will wrap around your home and your loved ones; even your neighborhood and your community will feel the impact. You can't stop it. It isn't you; it's him. He will be drawing people to himself and changing the world through how he made you. This is the way the surrendered life works and multiplies in his hands. Not when we have everything that we want or when all of our questions are answered, but today. And as women begin to wake up alongside you, they may want to thank you for being authentic or for being a catalyst for their journey; just smile and say thank you. Then later, on your knees, give God thanks and praise for the way he's using you to change your world.

9

Enrich Your Relationships

She stood at the altar, dressed in white, a vision of pure loveliness. When the minister asked the bride the most important question, she softly whispered, "I do." She looked lovingly at her intended and squeezed his hand. He smiled. When asked the same question, the groom replied, "I do." She turned to him and said, "Why did you say it like that?"

The hardest part about relationships is being *in* them. If we could just observe and analyze them, or simply talk about our intentions for them, we would all be relationship experts. Most of us are experts on other people's relationships. We know exactly what *they* should do and why *they* should do it. But when it comes to our own relationships, um, that's a different matter. We aren't so objective. We don't see our own patterns as clearly as we see those of others. We can spot someone else's addiction a mile away—but our own? Much harder to see and acknowledge.

Author Charlie Shedd says he encountered this difficulty when he first wrote about parenting. He wrote and taught parents the "Ten Commandments for Raising Perfect Kids." Then he had his first child. His list soon became "Ten Hints for Parents," followed by "A Few Tentative Suggestions for Fellow Strugglers"—after his second child. By the time his third child came along, he had stopped speaking on the subject.

Gary Smalley believes that women have a built-in understanding of relationships that men don't have. I have heard him refer to this understanding as an internal manual. Women seem to know what can help a relationship get better. We are blessed with an ability to nurture and meet needs in a way that men don't naturally think about. *Yay!* for our knowing.

Unfortunately, knowing and doing are two separate things.

It's one thing to talk about the negative effect of insecurity in a relationship; it's another to deal with your own insecurities. It's important to encourage forgiveness in marriage; it's excruciatingly painful when you have something to forgive. What could be more critical than stressing the rewards of good communication? Yet when feelings are hurt or respect is withheld, communicating honestly can be the last thing on your mind. Knowing what to do is easy. Doing it presents the real challenge.

What can move us from understanding to practicing? From knowing to doing? What can keep us from reading this chapter and saying, "I know this"? The truth is, we do know this. We "know" too much. Women can "know" their way into jealous rages, critical spirits, hard hearts, destructive patterns, torrid affairs, and bitter divorces.

To "know" alone, will never bring change. As long as the *knowledge of* remains separated from the *living out*, we will struggle between knowing and doing, between understanding and healing. You can know everything and do nothing.

For fun, I looked up the word *know* in my thesaurus. Here are the words I found: *understand, think, comprehend, discern, fathom, trust, grasp, look at, notice, observe, perceive, realize, recognize, see, take in, view, espy, assume, conceive, estimate, gather, imagine, infer, suppose,* and *suspect.*

Guess what? You can understand, think, comprehend, discern, and fathom without giving. You can grasp, look at, notice, observe, and perceive without caring. You can recognize, see, take in, view, espy, and assume without ever loving. And it's not a problem to conceive, estimate, gather, infer, suppose, or suspect without ever actually doing anything.

Relationships that exist in our heads don't touch our hands or our hearts.

Perhaps this is why our relationships are in such trouble. Henri Nouwen wrote, "While the desire for love has seldom been so directly expressed, love in its daily appearance has seldom looked so broken. While in our intensely competitive society the hunger and thirst for friendship, intimacy, union, and communion are immense, it never has been so difficult to satisfy this hunger and quench this thirst."

Perhaps we know too much. We read too many books and watch too many talk shows and hear too many sermons without putting one thing into practice. Could knowledge be killing our relationships? At the end of the day, after two talk shows, a Dobson program, and a conversation with your know-it-all neighbor, when you've yelled at your kids, said mean things to your husband, or forgotten to follow through on something you told a friend you would do, you must ask yourself this question: "What principle, theory, or way of thinking will ever change my life unless I put it into practice?"

Knowledge is not the key to great relationships. Knowing all the principles can help if we use them, but otherwise they profit us nothing. Because it is simply not enough to know.

In creating my aforementioned thesaurus list, one particular word caught my attention. In all the grasping, comprehending, noticing, perceiving, there was a word that didn't fit, one word for *know* that called me to something more than my brain: *trust*. This is the bridge. Trust is what makes knowledge count in relationships. If our knowing moves toward trusting, then it will make a difference in our relationships. Otherwise, it is only knowing. You can't trust your way to divorce. You can't trust your way into a jealous rage. You can't trust your way to insecurity.

Trust moves us out of our knowing into doing. To trust God moves us from knowing about God to knowing God. To trust is to depend on, rely on, bank on, build on, count on. All pretty much action words. You must move out of your head and into your heart in order to trust. You cannot depend on someone or build on something with mere knowledge. The words call us to action, not just inspection. The word *on* is significant as well. You can't merely rely. You can't just depend. You can't build without something to build *on*. Trust comes with a requirement of something or someone that moves us out of our heads, away from merely thinking and confidently into doing. Trust holds the feet of knowledge to the fire of action.

This chapter is our ninth cup of fresh-brewed life. Each previous cup had less to do with others and more to do with ourselves. You embrace your beauty without waiting for someone else to embrace it first; you encounter your journal whether anybody pats you on the back or not; you interview your anger for what it teaches you; then you learn to apply it to your relationships.

> **Marriage is our last, best chance to grow up.**
> —Joseph Barth

Now we take a closer look at how living a fresh-brewed life will enrich your relationships. We'll look at several of the cups that we have sought to draw from and incorporate their truths into the realm of our relationships, to enrich them by increasing this desirable quality: trust. Enriching our relationships with trust is like adding vitamin C to orange juice or fortifying milk with vitamin D. It provides more nourishment and enhances what is already present.

This is the invitation to move beyond *knowing* the principles of good relationships to *trusting* them to work for you, to learning to trust others with what you are experiencing in your life; to move from understanding a fresh-brewed life to living it out in the presence of those we love.

Directed Journaling

- Does trusting come easily for you? Write why you think you struggle with trust, or why you think it comes easily for you.
- Pick two of the chapters that we have walked through and write in detail what you can do to put more trust in those areas of your relationship.

Enrich Your Relationship with God

The more we choose to trust God's love, the more it will change our hearts and lives. Not trusting God's love doesn't make it any less true. It simply makes it untrue for us. It keeps us locked out of the freedom God's embrace could bring to our lives. It's like being invited to a party you decide not to attend: the party will go on without you, and should bitterness or mistrust in your own heart keep you away, you are the one who loses. You could have been at the party having the time of your life.

Intellectual understanding of our position in Christ will

not change us unless we learn to *trust* that identity in the daily encounters we have with God. Many of us had a mental understanding or even a belief that our parents loved us, but because our experiences hinted at a different truth, it fell short of bringing us a solid foundation for our identity or a confidence in launching out toward more intimacy. Because we could not seek to love others from a safe place of the love we'd received, we often looked to others to give us the love we'd longed for.

There is no fear in love. But perfect love drives out fear.

—1 John 4:18

No woman enters a relationship thinking this is what she is doing. This terribly painful insight usually follows another deep relational disappointment. We may feel betrayed or lonely or dissatisfied, and only then will we be confronted by how much we depended on the relationship to make us whole, to provide something more than a relationship can ever provide—an identity.

If you are in a relationship with someone who begins to pull away, you may be faced with strong feelings of rejection that cause you to question your worth. How much of your identity did you build on that relationship? With the possibility of losing that person, you realize that you trusted him for more than companionship or intimacy. You trusted him to complete you.

We do find a *sense* of completion in relationship. We are drawn to those who possess qualities that we don't have. We long to find someone who fits us and makes us feel "whole." It can feel incredibly satisfying to think you've found the person to complete you. Unfortunately, the satisfying part of this false "completion" lasts through the courtship or the early marriage. Should we enter into relationship to take away loneliness, we will discover quickly that it doesn't work so well. It's like two ticks with no dog—each trying to get from the other what it

Fresh-Brewed Adventures

- Go to a nice restaurant, or just stay in, but find a quiet place to spend an evening with your spouse or boyfriend, talking about the good things in your relationship. Discuss the cups of fresh-brewed life. Ask which one he would like to see enriching more of your relationship. Just listen; you may be surprised by what he says.
- Spend some time journaling about your current relationship or about your marriage. What principle will ever change your life until you commit to do it? What does your relationship need more of? How can you begin to make the necessary changes? Begin with prayer for God's help.
- Celebrate your relationship with a party. Plan something fun. Use the suggestions for celebration from the friendship chapter and go all out. Not expensive, not a lot of people, necessarily—just make sure you have the things that count.

needs to fill itself up. The only thing worse than being single and lonely is being married and lonely.

Giving ourselves to a relationship with God affords us the opportunity to enter a relationship that will change our patterns and our hearts. God's love is strong enough to complete as much of us as can be completed—another person is not only not a strong enough base but also it is an idolatry that will break our hearts.

Enrich Your Relationships—Interview Anger

Hopefully you are on your way to becoming the Barbara Walters of your soul. Whenever you find fear or frustration or hurt feelings, you are taking note and trying to get to the bottom of it. You are asking yourself good questions and seeking to answer them honestly. You can rest assured you will change your relationships if you trust this principle in your own life.

But there is more: gently offer this cup of fresh-brewed life to those around you. If you have learned to interview your own anger or you are committed to trying, then try the same process with those you care about. Ask thoughtful, probing questions that can help others take a closer look at the CHECK ENGINE SOON lights on their dashboards.

A very important note here: you cannot help anyone else with his or her anger if you are still dealing with your own. It takes softness and tenderness to ask the kind of questions needed. Try to move loved ones to a place of uncovering the tender hurt they have experienced. While you can't always ask someone else, "Where does it hurt?"—to keep that question in your mind could lead you to some other good questions that can help you guide that person to the wounded place.

The interview process is a critical tool for good communication. The quicker we can get to the heart of any issue, the more quickly and painlessly it can be resolved. Marriages, friendships, and churches can be torn apart by minor issues causing deep wounds. It's the "hard hurt" that causes these wounds. The sooner we are able get underneath them to the real pain, the more honestly the pain can be dealt with and potentially healed. A well-placed interview question can change the course of an evening, a retreat, or a board meeting. The battle route leaves people bloody for days, even years, while dealing with the real hurt will bring peace and growth.

Enriching Your Relationships by Encountering Your Journal

Journaling is like free counseling for your relationship. To the degree that journaling helps us ferret out the negative, destructive voices in our souls, it will only help our relationships. When we bring a more awake, authentic, living self to any relationship, satisfaction is increased tenfold. When we bring our hearts to God on paper and spill out our souls before him, it will impact every relationship we have. If we are learning from our lives by listening, responding, and letting God direct us, every special person in our lives will reap incredible benefits.

For example, many times after a conflict, my journal is the place where I conduct the interview. As I am fuming or crying, I need a place to process. I begin to write over and over how wrong I felt someone was, how it went, how mad she made me, how I don't plan to forgive her, and on the twelfth time, I see plain as day how wrong I was. I peel back another layer and write about what I did and perhaps why I did it. Sometimes I have to ask God to show me why I said what I said or did what I did. If I don't wrestle it out in my journal, I can easily miss what I did wrong or, more significantly, the reason I did it. The latter is what I am after. For me to see it and understand why I did whatever I did is pretty critical to it not happening again (at least not in the next twenty-four hours).

God has access to my heart through my journal. He meets me in the midst of my writing, and he teaches me about relationship. It is in my journal that I wrestle with issues of forgiveness. It is in my writing time that I pray for those I love. God brings things to my mind that I can pray for. Journaling is a structured way to pray for your loved ones, and we know that when we begin to pray, God does amazing things.

Enriching Your Relationship by Changing Your World Together

Henri Nouwen wrote, "Marriage is foremost a vocation. Two people are called together to fulfill the mission that God has given them. That is to say, a man and a woman come together for life, not just because they experience deep love for each other, but because they believe that God loves each of them with an infinite love and has called them to each other to be living witnesses of that love."

There is something very compelling in watching a couple working side by side, shoulder to shoulder. When they demonstrate love and respect for each other, they demonstrate God's love for the world. As ever, this happens far more by what they do than by what they say. To stand together with another individual in love—with one mission, purpose, and passion—this is a beautiful sight to behold. This is also a powerful force for change in the world.

Love does not consist in gazing at each other, but in looking together in the same direction.

—Antoine de Saint-Exupéry

We show God's love to each other in relationship. When we forgive someone, this is a sign of God's forgiveness of us. We are never more like God than when we forgive others. Relationships afford us our greatest opportunity to model the gospel. We are called to be light-bearers in a dark world that only recognizes one language: love. The Scriptures tell us that the world will only recognize us as followers of Christ by the love that we have for one another.

Have you ever prayed about your mission as a couple? If you have been fortunate enough to discover your passion in life, your "one thing" in serving God, you can be a great encouragement to your spouse or friends to keep seeking their "one thing" as well.

Many times a mission comes from combining your passion with those in your circle. Whether it is teaching a Bible study together, hammering with Habitat for Humanity to build houses, or just going on an overseas trip together to work—something electric happens when we combine forces. One plus one no longer equals just two; it multiplies exponentially.

Enriching Your Relationship by Listening to Your Longings

I had my wisdom teeth taken out a number of years ago. They were impacted in my jaw and causing me headaches and pain. When an impacted tooth is extracted, it leaves a gaping hole. I left the surgeon's office with four rather large holes in my head. I had pain medicine and a list of instructions from the doctor. I don't remember much about that day, as I spent all of it in bed. But around 8:00 p.m., I awoke to searing, throbbing, aching pain. My head was on fire. I took more medicine, but it didn't help. I had not slept much when I crawled back to the doctor the next morning. I just knew I'd developed some rare disease in the night and he would have to remove my face to stop the pain. I'd made peace with it.

Turns out what I'd developed was neither a disease nor rare. It was a common condition called *dry socket*. Lovely, right? The places in my jaw where my wisdom teeth had lived were now dry, howling holes. The pain was, um, well . . . intense. The kind of pain that wraps around your ears, pushes behind your eyes, keeps you from walking straight, and makes you say very mean things to anyone in earshot. To alleviate the pain, the oral surgeon mercifully inserted a long, clove-saturated gauze. As soon as the holes were filled with this gauze, they stopped screaming. The pain subsided instantly. It would have been a miracle cure, except for the taste of cloves. The clove mixture was so strong I felt sick to my stomach. I was thankful that the merciless throbbing was gone. Nothing, not even this horrible taste, was worse than that ache. So I was grateful, but I did swear off cloves. To this day, I can't eat much that has been flavored with cloves without gagging. (Interesting how I can manage pumpkin pie).

Unfortunately, the holes can't heal with the gauze stuck in there. Eventually the stuffing must come out, and the holes must be left empty for a while to heal. I wished that someone would invent the kind of gauze that would just dissolve inside those sockets—and while they were at it, make it taste like chocolate mousse.

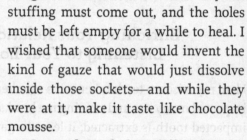

> If you cannot inspire a woman with love of you, fill her above the brim with love of herself; all that runs over will be yours.
> —Charles Caleb Colton

I went through three different cycles of dry socket, stuff the holes, choke on the cloves, peace, remove the gauze, screaming jaw pain . . . stuff, choke, peace . . . By the third time, I had this insight about the human soul: we all have holes in us. Profound, I know. When we keep the holes full—with cloves or clothes, food, activity, etc.—they don't howl, but they don't heal. And if we are blessed enough to grow weary of the bitter taste of stuffing things into the empty places inside us, we must prepare our hearts for the difficulty journey toward healing. It will involve pain because when we remove the things we've used to "medicate" our empty places, we ache deeply, and the howling is loud and strong. But the Great Physician walks with us and holds us in our pain until the temptation to keep stuffing gives way to the reality of the healing.

Enrich Your Relationship by Celebrating Friendship

The number one reason women have affairs is friendship. Not the "Let's go the mall" variety, but a deep and abiding sense of companionship and enjoyment of the other's presence. While girlfriends offer friendship to us that a man cannot (and should not), to exclude friendship with your mate because you only find it with your girlfriends will hurt your relationship. The friendship with our spouses needs to be cultivated and celebrated as well. If the friendship dies in your marriage, it's going to be tough sledding to maintain a healthy, lifelong relationship. If you want to affair-proof your marriage, make sure you are having fun together on a daily (or at least weekly) basis. This may mean it's up to us to get the party started, but the effort will bring great rewards.

Once in relationship, many men tend to slack off in the pursuit of friendship with their wives. I don't know if this is a retro characteristic that goes back to their caveman days, but for some reason they don't seem to pursue us as much after "I do." However, their trust level seems to increase. While we may feel taken for granted, they

> **We always deceive ourselves about the people we love—first to their advantage, then to their disadvantage.**
>
> —Albert Camus

are trusting in their way. Regardless of whose fault it is, if the friendship in your marriage wanes, nurturing and enriching it with trust will ensure it has the best chance to thrive.

Enrich Your Relationship by Embracing Your Beauty

There is no question that strikes fear in the heart of man quicker than "How does this look on me?" Their spines go numb, and they feel anxious and tingly all over. They inspect the floor and their footwear and any object of interest that might be down there. They shift their weight and brush lint off the sleeves of their jackets. It's a setup, and every man knows it.

Men are in a tough spot because they can't win one way or the other. We are looking to them to ease our fears or reassure us or confirm our worst fears. "Do these pants make my butt look big?" How in the world can a man answer that question? It's not even an honest question. Maybe you do have a generous rear end; that's okay, but what are you really asking him? We'd really like to blame men for how we feel about ourselves. We set them up to fail, and when they do, we are frustrated. We can change this.

Learning to embrace (make peace with) how we look moves us from setting them up to setting them free. It's a God issue more than a man issue. Beauty, many men have communicated, ultimately comes from a woman's confidence and trust in her worth. Even men know they cannot handle the weight of determining a woman's worth. It creates fear, and frankly, it should. We cannot trust men to help us embrace our sense of beauty if we are trusting *in* them to determine our worth.

The path of enriching our relationships is a way of trust and the only road that leads us from knowing to loving. Trust does not come naturally to us. Almost all of us have a story of how our trust was broken at some point and why we struggle to trust others. After all, this issue of trust was the first breach in the garden. The question arose in the heart of Eve, *Should I trust God?* Heartbreaking as it turned out to be, she opted not to, which changed her relationship with God, as it does ours when we make the same choice.

You may be asking, what about people who aren't trustworthy? *Am I supposed to trust someone who has let me down?*

The first step in learning to trust others is seeking to become a trustworthy person. Usually when we have a pattern of not trusting, it is for one of two reasons: (1) we mistrust others because we don't trust ourselves, or (2) we have made poor choices when we have trusted in the past. When we take the steps to become a person who can be trusted, we can begin to change our pattern of not trusting. You will begin to trust yourself, and you'll know what qualities to look for in determining someone else's trustworthiness.

This is not to say we will not be scarred in the process of learning to trust. Trusting can be bloody. When Jacob wrestled with the angel, he was learning to trust, and it left him limping. Often in our battle to trust, we have to wrestle with our deepest, darkest, worst fears. We must wrestle them to the ground, and then we trust. For example, if you are trying to trust God for financial provision, ask yourself, *What is the worst thing that could happen?* Could you still trust God if that happened? If you can wrestle that fear to the ground and know that God is still there in the quietness of the dark, then you are on your way to trusting on a whole new level.

When we trust others, we reveal that we have learned to trust God at a deep level. Trusting others also reveals that we have come to trust ourselves. We have not placed our hope solely in others' trustworthiness. We have placed our hope in a Savior who is completely able to come through for us and meet our needs. We do not demand demonstrations of another's ability to be trusted, although we are discerning about this, because our ultimate trust is not in other people. We understand with compassion that people will disappoint and frustrate, but we can choose to believe their hearts toward us are good. When we intentionally enrich every relationship with this kind of trust, we move from knowing about a fresh-brewed life to living it and reaping the rewards on a daily basis.

10

Enjoy Your Freedom

A mother was trying to explain to her bored little girl what her own childhood had been like. "We used to skate outside on a pond. We had a swing made from a big tire that hung from a tree in our front yard, and we would play on that for hours. We rode our pony. We picked wild raspberries in the woods." The little girl was wide-eyed, taking this all in. At last she said to her mother, "I sure wish I'd gotten to know you sooner!"

Ever wonder if your kids or friends might feel that way? Where have we gone as we've "grown up"? Have we "grown" in ways that might not be growth at all? Sometimes we describe not growing as feeling "stuck." But what if, worse than stuck, we actually shrink? What if, held in captivity by our adult taskmasters, our hearts actually shrink and get smaller? Dulled by our responsibilities, if life has gone out of our lives, we might actually be diminishing in our capacity for freedom and joy. When starving yourself of food, your stomach will feel as though it has shrunk (whether physically it has or not), and eating what you once did no longer feels comfortable. Such must be the case if we've lost our ability to play and lose ourselves in the enjoyment of our surroundings or our relationships. Who wants to grow up if it means we're not free to play anymore?

Oh, to walk daily in the freedom of Christ. To care much less about what others think or how we might appear to them and instead put the bulk of our focus on the joy offered to us in the abundant life Christ promised. How do we appear to our heavenly Father? As free and loving children, basking in the incomparable, but broken, world in which he has placed us? Or as stressed, overextended people-pleasers unable to enjoy his lavish provision?

Familiar Prisons

By most standards, Brooks Hatlen is not a very significant character in the history of film. Not many people could place his name or even call to mind the actor who played him, but some, like me, will never forget his role in *The Shawshank Redemption*. Hatlen, played by James Whitmore, is a crusty but lovable old inmate who runs the prison library.

Brooks keeps his pet bird, Jake, in the pocket of his droopy blue cardigan. He cares for Jake and feeds him from the prison scraps discarded by his friends. Then one day, the unthinkable happens—Brooks's parole comes through. The old man goes berserk and holds a knife at another prisoner's throat because, he explains, "It's the only way they'd let me stay."

> Those who desire to give up freedom in order to gain security will not have, nor do they deserve, either one.
>
> —Benjamin Franklin

Why in the world would anyone when offered a chance for freedom not desperately want it? Just asking the question about

Brooks's behavior quickly turned a spotlight on my own. Sad to say, it wasn't all that hard to think of several past examples where I had chosen prisons of my own making because they were comfortable, small, and familiar. All I had to do was look back through my own journey of waking up to remember many of the cells I once called home.

The prison of insecurity. I spent years—okay, decades—worrying about what people might be thinking about me. Churning inside with anxiety over how I was doing or, more accurately, how others might be thinking I was doing. I found it far easier to conclude that they thought the worst of me than to ask how they felt or to trust them to think whatever they liked, even if it might be wrong. I was stuck in a prison of looking for my worth in the eyes of others, trying to discern their thinking. As it turns out, "they" weren't thinking about me at all.

The prison of anger. Inadequate as a girl to process the sadness that was my childhood companion and not free to express much outward anger in my family, I had more fuel dumps in my soul than Saudi Arabia. It wasn't until I found my voice and could give words to my sadness that I could see how my anger was a by-product of repressed emotion. I could only contain my feelings for so long, and then someone would throw a match into my cell, and the whole thing would explode. But when the dust settled and the smoke cleared, the door was still locked, and I was still behind bars, unable to go free. Finally the day came when the fuel dumps had been painfully drained, the dry, brittle underbrush that easily caught fire had been cleared away, and I looked up, tired from the cleaning going on in my cell, wiped my sweaty brow (or my cheeks) of tears only to notice that the door now hung open.

The prison of work. While hard work has its virtues, and I'm the first to trot them out in self-defense, I've been very guilty of locking myself in a cell of work. Bound by a need to prove my worth, by a fear of not looking busy enough, and even by the

Enjoy Your Freedom   173

uncertainty of what I would do if I stopped working, I labored unhealthily for many years. Work conveniently provided a small and very familiar cell to me that I lived in for so long, there was a time after freedom had come that I didn't think I could work unless I locked myself in it again. The voice of the cell inside me would whisper things like:

- If you goof off and don't get to work, you're never going to get anything done.
- Look how hard so-and-so is working; you're already way behind.
- People don't think you have a "real" job; you need to convince them.

From the vantage point of these cells, with or without a window, freedom felt like some strange, unknown land and, had I tried to say it out loud, a land I feared might not even exist. I heard people talk about it, saw a few remarkable people who looked as though they knew what freedom was, but because I wasn't sure what I would do with it, I just stayed locked up— until my wake-up call, those unrelenting longings, propelled me in search of a better way.

In the story of Shawshank, Brooks's friend Red, played by Morgan Freeman, sadly describes Brooks as "institutionalized" because the old man had been on the inside for fifty years. "This is all he knows. In here, he's an important man; he's an educated man. Outside he's nothin'—just a used-up con with arthritis in both hands. Probably couldn't get a library card if he tried . . . These walls are funny. First you hate 'em, then you get used to 'em. Enough time passes, it gets so you depend on 'em . . . They send you here for life, and that's exactly what they take. The part that counts anyways."

Our journey toward a fresh-brewed life culminates in deep

and lasting freedom—learning to be free from destructive patterns, learning to have healthy relationships free of enslaving insecurities, and learning to be free in our relationship with God, trusting him with all that we have and all that we are. It's a journey that requires—what else?—honesty and commitment to our own freedom. We all have "prisons" of our own making, some we've already stepped out of and others for which we've not yet discovered the keys. But a promise of freedom isn't worth anything, really, not even the cost of the paper in this book to those who are unwilling to hope they could be free. Just like Brooks, such individuals risk becoming institutionalized, unable to walk in freedom because they've come to see freedom as the enemy and their prison as freedom.

After his "attempt" to lengthen his sentence and stay in prison fails, Brooks is released. The film follows Brooks through his new life on the "outside." He finds work as a grocery bagger at the Foodway and finds shelter at a halfway house for inmates just getting out of prison. The world is a faster, louder, more complex place than Shawshank. Brooks is lonely and disoriented. It is painfully clear he can't find his place in a free world. He can't sleep and contemplates committing another crime just to be sent back to prison, but he decides he's too old. Brooks narrates, "I don't like it here. I'm tired of being afraid all the time. I've decided not to stay." As we hear his words read from a letter to his friends in prison, we see him climb onto a chair, then onto a table . . . and Brooks Hatlen kicks the table out from under the weight of his heavy life and hangs himself.

Freedom can be more dangerous than prison. Red's philosophy rings true about walls. First we hate them, then we become used to them, and then we need them. Brooks Hatlen could not survive freedom, as heartbreaking as this truth is. He had been in prison too long to make his freedom count for anything. Brooks needed the walls.

And so do some of us.

When the apostle Paul wrote in Galatians 5:1 that Christ set us free so that we could be free, it sounds like some sort of scriptural double-talk. But looking at the life of Brooks Hatlen, we can see it isn't double-talk at all. In fact, Paul was putting words around a very frightening truth. Even religion, the very thing that people look to for freedom, can be enslaving. He was warning his Galatian readers, and us, that Christ can set us free, but without careful attention, we can still choose slavery.

The apostle Paul had found in Christ a joyous freedom from the suffocating laws of religion. This was the kind of freedom he preached (and I can only imagine, embodied) wherever he traveled. When he wrote this letter, the Galatian church was retreating back inside the "safe walls" of religion because they were afraid of the kind of freedom Paul taught. It made them uncomfortable; they didn't "get" grace because it didn't feel right to them.

In a sense these early believers were "institutionalized." They had grown comfortable in a religion of slavery where they'd been imprisoned by the "rules" and had lost sight (not to mention the hope) of real freedom. They confused freedom with what was comfortable to them, what they had known before they had been set free—attempts to earn God's approval. Paul warned them sternly that this was a trap, that freedom was a deeper issue than just what felt comfortable. The Galatians didn't want to hear it. Yet Paul never backed down, writing even stronger things, like, "O foolish Galatians, who has bewitched you? Who is telling you that what you were offered in Christ by grace, you can now finish with rules?" (Gal. 3:1, paraphrased). In essence, he was pleading with them: "Why are you setting aside your freedom to go back to prison?"

What a great question, and not just for first-century Christians. This is a question we should ask ourselves often. Where are we settling for slavery over freedom, and why? While the answers may seem simple on the surface, lasting solutions are not. If it were just a matter of physical freedom, why would a woman who has faced repeated abuse return to the clutches of a destructive relationship? What makes a soul prefer the confines and restrictions of harsh captivity to the wide-open space and choices of amazing and glorious freedom? Why do we need the walls?

An Inside Job

A prison cell holds us when the issue that created the imprisonment has a hold over us. Somewhere along the road of our lives, we were presented with a lie, and we chose to believe it, giving it power. This belief may have been conscious, subconscious, or unconscious, but that lie deep inside us creates slavery. All lies do, even small ones. Only by replacing the lie with the truth as deep inside as we are able, and putting our emotional and intellectual weight down on it, will we be set free.

Sound simple? Think it through. While the truth is still true if no one believes it, a lie becomes as strong as a truth even if only one person, you, believes it to be so. When you believe a lie—like, you are only worth as much or as little as what is in your savings account—it might as well be true. In fact, you make it true in your life. Then it has power, and you are locked in a prison of your own making. Until the lie is replaced, you can only feel as good as your money says you can.

These are the harshest prisons because no one can let us out. We might ask others, and often do, to release us, convincing them that they have the "keys" to our cells. Others, well-meaning and not, may even lead us to believe they can release us. Not possible. To trust this is to step foolishly into a different kind of slavery by believing another lie. Real freedom would be found in that house or in that husband or by finally having that something we have been unable to have.

Therapists, friends, family, strangers, furry animals, all may illuminate aspects of our prison and help reveal lies we've believed, but until we understand the shape of our own individual locks, real freedom will never be ours. Unfortunately, this work can only be done in prison, in essence, on the "inside," in order to step out into the fresh air of real life. This freedom cannot be bestowed on us. This kind of freedom is created in us, while we are still prisoners.

Even the most glorious freedom available, the release from the penalty and punishment of sin, made possible by Jesus himself, cannot be ours by mere pronouncement. The truth that Christ died for us while we were yet sinners does not become ours until it meets us in the corner of our dark, stinky cells, wraps around our minds, permeating our souls, saturating our hearts until we can lift our eyes from the dirt and see the way out. Even Christ, who did all he could humanly and divinely do to rescue us, cannot make us walk, live, or enjoy our freedom. He can only make it possible for us to do so and, by his grace, believe that we can.

Declawing the Lies

So what still holds you back? Will hearing once again that freedom really is possible get through to your heart this time? Not if you still believe lies at your core. As you read the two lies that follow, consider whether you have embraced either one. Both lived deep in my mind and heart before I found my way free.

Lie: You are not to be trusted.

In believing this lie, we tell ourselves that freedom is really no good for us. Why, we might go off the deep end and do something crazy. Like most lies that hold our hearts, this one starts early. We believe it first, not because we wanted to, but because someone told us this was true. By their words or actions, a parent, a sibling or a relative communicated, "I don't trust you to do the right thing. You are not capable of good choices." Maybe someone said (after you made a mistake), "*Now* look what you've done. Clearly you can't handle this freedom, and I won't give it to you again." So we tuck away what we've heard, even if we don't want it to be true, and the lie lives inside us, keeping us in an environment with high control. Otherwise, we reason, we'll get into real trouble. This lie will feel correct, in part (as all good lies do) at least for a while, until we long to get free from that voice. Sometimes this requires us to go back to the breakfast table, where we spilled the juice we were trying to pour, to reveal the lie we've spent way too long believing. It's there that we can swap the lie for the truth that you can spill juice or even get pregnant when you're sixteen without having to spend the rest of your life in jail.

Lie: Failure is unforgivable.

If you were shamed for failing, whatever the failure may have been, there's a good chance you'll go to great lengths to keep from feeling that way again. Some go so far as to create different prisons of lying, blaming, working, or pretending, simply to avoid feelings of failure. When a parent is deeply disappointed in a child's behavior, that child has great difficulty believing the parent is not disappointed in her as a person. She grows up believing the lie that she is a disappointment to others. Not too surprisingly, this child may spend many years just disappointing others. She remains stuck, feeling locked away by this awful truth, which is not a truth at all, while the real truth remains true, but on the other side of a door with no handle. So she lives and makes choices right out of that lie that she has chosen for her life. *Failure is inevitable, so it would be stupid of me to try. Why try and fail?* She (or he) subconsciously finds a comfortable pattern in the parent's house, in the military service, in an abusive marriage, or even in a state penitentiary, somewhere the now adult can disappoint constantly, all the while despising the rules but needing the walls.

These awful lies are insidious because they attach deeply to our souls before we can thoughtfully decide whether or not they are true. Our souls learn to fear freedom while longing for it at the same time. We are confused, and instead of pressing through until we can get the kind of clarity that would move us toward freedom, we settle in and redecorate our cells.

Hopefully, by this chapter, our alive, awake souls can more easily recognize what it means to settle for captivity and will sternly (if possible) resist the temptation to do so. Because living in and enjoying real freedom in our lives won't just happen. We must pursue freedom intentionally, trusting, as in the other cups of this book, that over time we will see the results we've hoped and prayed for.

So if you're ready to taste greater freedom in your life, these important components will help you achieve freedom, order your freedom, and maintain it for the rest of your life.

The Price of Freedom

Those of us fortunate enough to live in America know very personally from our history that freedom has a price. In breaking away from England, the colonists had to work to secure their liberty, and the cost was high. America had to win the right to govern herself. The freedom these colonists sought would never have just happened; it had to be fought for and won. And so it goes for each freedom we seek personally. It usually requires that a battle be fought or a price be paid, depending on the type of freedom we're seeking.

As adult women, we must secure the freedom to make our own choices. Interestingly enough, we can actually believe we possess this self-determination when, in fact, we do not. Ask yourself honestly how much inner conflict in your life is created around decisions you don't feel the freedom to make. Who is making the decisions that govern your life? Think about how you decide where you'll spend the holidays or how you will discipline your children. Do you ever feel pressure from your family or friends to make choices other than the ones you feel are best?

If you've ever struggled with addiction, you know—up close and personal—that there is a battle to be fought before freedom can be yours. If you've ever formed a friendship with someone who is codependent, it can be very difficult to regain your independence. Should you try to curb that unhealthy friendship, you will pay a price to do so. There is not one freedom, big or small, involving countries or hearts, that comes without cost or without struggle. If you desire to be free, you have to be willing to go to battle for it.

> **Freedom is never voluntarily given by the oppressor; it must be demanded by the oppressed.**
>
> —Martin Luther King Jr.

This doesn't mean that you have to intentionally wound people or leave carnage in your wake to secure your own freedom at any price. It means that when you desire more freedom, more emotional health, more autonomy, you must adjust your expectations to prepare for the cost and quite possibly the pain. However, the better you are able to handle the conflict and the clearer you can be about your motive (simply freedom in love), the easier it will be to heal and recover.

The Plan for Freedom

Once America won her freedom, a new challenge began. How would we order this freedom so our new country could stay

Fresh-Brewed Adventures

- Visit a museum exhibit dedicated to some aspect of freedom. Bring your journal, and let the exhibit speak to your life and inspire you to move toward one new freedom.
- Make a point to visit someone in prison. Generally, if you haven't done this before, it could take several weeks to get cleared, so start the process and follow through on a day you set aside. Pray every day leading up to your visit for an open heart and open eyes. It will touch your life and the life of the one you go to see.
- If you have trouble allowing others to pay for a meal, make a point to allow a friend to take you to lunch without trying to pick up the check or feeling bad that you're not contributing. Spend some time writing in your journal after lunch about the kind of freedom it takes to receive.

free? The Constitution and the Bill of Rights were painstakingly crafted and put into place to establish how America would order the sovereignty she'd fought so hard to achieve.

In our lives now, we must look ahead and ask, what will we do with our freedom once we've gained it? How will we order it? How will we make the most of it to enjoy it? Whether you are trying to end a bad relationship or gain control over your unruly closet, you must make a plan for what happens after you have gotten what you're fighting for. It's crucial for your success.

Visualizing the potential our freedom can hold makes us stronger in fighting for it and more willing to pay the price to obtain it. It moves freedom out of the realm of some unknown territory and into the reality of what we will actually do when we have it. If I am taming my wild closet, once I get it free of slithering belts and mismatched shoes, if I don't know what I'm going to do differently going forward or how I plan to handle daily dirty laundry, I won't have a clean closet for long. We order our freedom so that we can stay free. When we plan what our new freedom will look like practically, the plan will clarify our first steps so we don't falter.

> To know how to free oneself is nothing; the arduous thing is to know what to do with one's freedom.
>
> —André Gide

For example, if a woman who has been abused dares to hope for a life free of violence, she must put feet to that hope of freedom by putting specific steps in place if she truly wants to be free. She pays the price, risking the wrath of her abuser, by calling the police, who separate her from the perpetrator. She can't simply "be free" yet. Studies show us that she needs a plan going forward or she'll be back with her abuser in no time. While the woman has taken a courageous first step toward freedom by fighting for it, without a strong plan for how she will order her freedom wisely, her familiar prison will still be warm when she returns. As painful as it is for us to admit, psychologists tell us the demons we know seem better than the ones we haven't met yet. Ask Brooks Hatlin.

So whether you're heading for the freedom of an "empty nest" or trying to figure out life after divorce or unlocking the door of a self-imposed prison, focus on the potential of the life in front of you and construct a plan, a fresh-brewed plan, for making the most of it once it is yours.

The Power of Freedom

The last component for fully establishing a freedom we can enjoy is to vigilantly maintain our freedom. Even after independence is yours and you're enjoying the life you've planned for and ordered, forces and factors may rise up again that threaten your self-determination. Boundaries you've worked hard to draw can get fuzzy over time. We have to keep an eye on enslaving habits that may encroach again, to maintain what we've worked so hard for. This is normal and expected, so don't let it derail your freedom train. For example, if you have done hard work with your parents to establish freedom for the way you intend to live, there may be setbacks as you progress. Evaluate them and do a little maintenance to keep the relationship from slipping back into bad patterns.

Freedom that is worth having needs to be maintained. A heart, much like a country or a garden, needs tending on a regular basis to keep it healthy and in good working order so it can grow. When its identity is established, ordered, and maintained, this land, garden, or heart will do what it was designed to do: produce great things from inside to offer to others. For the heart, living in true freedom will organically produce the fruit of the spirit: love, joy, peace, patience, kindness, goodness, faithfulness, gentleness, and self-control.

> There is no such thing as a little freedom. Either you are all free, or you are not free.
> —Walter Cronkite

To have a life marked by the abundance of this fruit is one of the great benefits of having paid the price and made your plan. This life is really good. Its freedom is the opposite of prison, with its cold concrete, scarce resources, and stark walls. It is lavish and sweet and full of warm love and flowing joy. Gone are the angry outbursts and the crippling insecurities; they've been recycled in God's amazing compost pile to produce the nutrients to grow the beautiful fruits. It is the restoration of what the starvation of prison took from your soul, fifty times over. And it's very "green."

A Day in the Life . . .

So what would enjoying real freedom look like on a regular basis? I began thinking about a day in the life of a truly free woman. Because everyone's life (and thus freedom) looks different, this is not a goal, a challenge, or a directive; this is a little piece of fiction that may spark some of your own thoughts about freedom. It is important to me that you know this is not my life. I'm still on the journey alongside you, and while I'm enjoying freedom more than I ever have, I still struggle to live free on a daily basis. So this is something I wrote to help me visualize what freedom on the inside might look like on the outside.

A Day in the Life of You as a Free Woman

Your alarm goes off, serving as an unwelcome reminder that you stayed up a little too late to watch the ending of a good movie. You feel tired, but instead of beating yourself up, you replay in your thoughts some nice moments of the movie as you brush your teeth.

As you are putting the water in the coffee pot, you decide not to complain about being tired, but instead, because you chose to watch the film, you're going to journal about what it added to your life.

At the breakfast table, amid the chaos of cereal and bickering, you resist an old pattern of yelling to try to get everyone in line and you simply stay calm and engaged with your children as you move them through the morning activities. Trying to focus on what they are doing right rather than what they are doing wrong is new and takes intentional thought, but it feels so much better as you drop them off at school. The genuine love you feel for them comes welling up inside you, and you realize it's been a while.

Sometime during the day you take a walk. Just a walk. Not an exercise break, just a "be with yourself" walk. You notice as you're studying the leaves turning that you've been walking for at least five minutes without worrying about your thighs, your weight, or what you ate or didn't eat for dinner last night—or how you're going to make it through the holidays without gaining ten pounds. This, too, is new.

Earlier you had a call with a friend that was so positive. There was no drama or conflict. There was no worry or anxiety that you may have offended someone or the need to speak of how you'd been offended, just meaningful, encouraging conversation. Peace.

At lunch you replied to an e-mail from your sister, who invited you to come for a visit next month during the kids' spring break. Normally, you would put off responding because of the difficulty of disappointing her with a no. Instead, you sit at your computer, ask God for words to convey your need to stay close to home that week, and push Send, trusting her to receive your heart. You find yourself surprised at how easy it was and how good it felt to simply tell the truth.

The afternoon was full of work, but it was an effort that had purpose and passion because you committed to do it, trusting the gifts that God has given you. Part of your time was spent in a conference room and the other part in your laundry room, but both brought satisfaction because you were free to bring yourself to the work.

A conversation with your elderly neighbor goes a little longer than anticipated, but you trust it was worth it and find a way to make up the time without stressing or second-guessing whether or not you should have invested. After all, you're free.

You listen to a voice mail on your phone, asking you to bring cookies for the class party in the morning. Frustrated and feeling taken advantage of, you put the butter out on the counter to start it softening while you look for what to fix for dinner. No eggs. So you realize you'll have to go to the store after dinner and wonder if you should just buy cookies instead of eggs. Something inside you feels bad about bringing store-bought cookies to the class party. Something also feels bad about getting a voice mail the night before they are needed. For the first time you can remember, you feel free to make either decision. You prepare dinner and make the choice to pick up cookies in the morning on the way to school.

After dinner, your five-year-old son offers his loudest protests about getting his bath. What has typically been an ordeal often ending in tears (mostly yours) ends instantly when you ask your son if he would like to skip his bath tonight and read books together in your bed instead. Overriding your mother's voice inside your head about being too permissive and the kind of child that will produce, you intentionally choose to listen instead to the voice of your little boy. But deeper than his voice, you hear his heart trying to tell you he needs more of your time and care. You climb into your bed with him and read books for an hour, encircled by peace and love.

Later, falling asleep you realize that your freedom led you to the right decision about the cookies. The time with your son was more valuable than presenting a better cookie offering tomorrow. You coach yourself and make a plan. When you show up with store-bought cookies in the morning, set them on the table and try not to look at all the other offerings. Instead, trust that you bought something money *can* buy so you could enjoy something money *can't* buy.

It was a great day in the life of you as a free woman.

Directed Journaling

- Looking back at your past, try to name three prisons of your own making, and explore their beginnings.
- Identify people you wanted to have the keys to your cells and put your thoughts down about what this taught you or revealed to you.
- Write some scenarios about what a day in your life would look like as a free woman.

Freedom never looks the same for every woman. In fact, it may look exactly opposite. Some women may begin to enjoy their freedom when they start saying no more frequently, while others will feel a new freedom to say yes to the invitations of others. By identifying honestly the places you are bound or held back, you will see more clearly where your freedom lies.

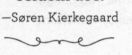

People demand freedom of speech as a compensation for the freedom of thought which they seldom use.

—Søren Kierkegaard

The circumstances of our lives do not determine our level of freedom. The level of self-governance we enjoy determines our response to the circumstances of our lives. There is a certain irony about the fact that the apostle Paul wrote some of his most compelling thoughts on freedom while in prison. He demonstrated that when we live out of the freedom of the "inner man," we are free regardless of how it may look on the outside.

We are not alone in our struggle to be free. We have help on the "inside" from Christ, who empowers us. After all, he is the one who paid the price for the freedom of our souls. He took on the sin that so easily entangles us, fought and defeated it, that we might know the freedom his love could bring. A love that sets us free to enjoy an abundant life with God, without anger or strife, free to serve others as they have need (without manipulation), free to cast and recast our heavy cares upon him because, more than all others, he cares for us.

Sometimes we fail to recognize this, like the Galatians or Brooks Hatlen, until the door slams behind us and we're back in a prison fashioned by the rules of our own making. Or even worse, we've lost hope for freedom and despair closes in, whispering that slavery is better anyway, and we might as well just settle in and get used to it. May it never be!

It is for freedom that Christ set us free. The kind of freedom that gives life, not takes it. The kind that tears walls down, not builds them up. Freedom based on truth unlocks the captive heart, mind, and spirit. So let God's love lift your heavy heart and hung-down head to show you the open door. Take your first steps of faith, and walk out in the sunlight. Trust with your whole being that when Christ sets you free, you are free indeed. Free for freedom. Walk in it. Run headlong into it. Play in the expanse of it. Laugh in the joy of it. Dance every day in delight of it.

Enjoy the freedom of your fresh-brewed life!

Epilogue

Good to the Last Drop

I closed the front door quietly and headed toward the waiting cab in the driveway. I looked down at a small pair of mud-choked cleats that lay where they'd been reluctantly removed the night before. I walked down the steps toward the driveway and noticed the snorkel left there by our fifteen-month-old daughter, who carries around her brother's prized possession like a trophy. It was early in the morning, and I was leaving on a short trip for work. The house behind me was quiet and sleeping, but in a few hours it would be anything but. The driver loaded my suitcase, and I surveyed the signs of life dotting the front porch and everywhere I looked. The gratitude that suddenly washed over me didn't miss a spot. I swallowed hard and took a couple of breaths to keep from crying.

Once inside the cab, I was on my knees in my heart, thanking God for the goodness and mercy that have been following me all the days of my life.

Two flights and a rental car later, I was in a circle of women who had been praying for me for over a year. They'd chosen me to be the speaker for their women's weekend. It was so evident that they had put their hearts into planning this event for the past many months. As we sat together in this circle the evening before the event, several of the women remarked that this had been the toughest year they'd had as a planning team. One of the women began to tell me some of the background.

Earlier that spring, the planners and volunteers for the weekend event had taken a retreat together. They'd never done this before. Shirley, the leader of the group, had set a block of time aside for each woman to share a little bit of what was happening in her life. Shirley had brought a large mound of clay and invited each woman to take a hunk of the clay to work in her hands while she was sharing. When they got the clay in their hands, they started kneading it and, before long, began opening up about their struggles. They shed tears of anguish over the pain in their lives and in the lives of those they loved and served. They laughed together at certain crazy parts in each other's stories and then prayed before putting (sometimes throwing) the hunk of clay back into the center when they were finished. The clay was worn-out, as was the woman telling her story.

I loved hearing about this way of sharing, and had the story ended there, it would have been a good one. But get this: after the retreat was over, Shirley took that hunk of worn-out clay to a local potter. The potter had no idea what the clay had been through or how many stories and tears it must have held. Following Shirley's instructions, the potter shaped the clay into several beautiful pieces.

The next time the leadership team got together, Shirley

presented them with a communion set that they would use together. The women were so touched when she presented them this beautiful offering, as was I, just listening to the story. I remember thinking how deep and powerful it was that this beautiful pottery had been made from the stories of their pain, their prayers, and their tears. My thoughts wandered to God collecting our tears. I had just started thinking about what he might be planning to do with them, when the woman who'd been sharing the story said to me, "Shirley had this piece made for you, Nicole." Suddenly, I was in their story as Shirley handed me a coffee mug, but so much more. "We've been praying for you and want you to have this for your morning coffee to remember the weekend theme of "Grounds for Hope."

The women in the circle had no way to know how deeply they'd ministered to me or how close my story had been to theirs. I held that valuable cup in my hands as my mind returned to the story I'm about to tell.

I began the journey of revising and expanding *Fresh-Brewed Life* with fear and trembling. Yet I welcomed the daunting task of reopening this dialogue I started over a decade ago. For some authors, ten-plus years might not bring so many updates—older kids, older face in the mirror, deeper wisdom, age-ripened joy. But for me, dear reader, almost every aspect of my life has changed. When *Fresh-Brewed Life* was first published, I was thirty-two years old, living in Tennessee, and married with no kids. I was awakening from a deep and painful sleep that had its gnarled roots in my young life. Much of this book was and still is a chronicle of that arduous and costly journey of waking up. It was a sorrowful and joyful process that I valued, then and now, almost as much as my own breath. While I wouldn't trade it even if such were possible, it would be untruthful to say I wouldn't mind going through it again. The joy in waking up propelled me into the sunlight with a zeal and zest for life I'd never known. But the same sunlight revealed dark truths better suited for those who choose to sleep. The realizations were the most painful of my adult life. Whatever the future might hold, I wasn't going back to the land of Nod. Ever. Without going into unnecessary details, my marriage ended. Anguish was multiplied by the years invested, and grief shook my heart like a dog with rag doll. A dark sense of failure closed in around me.

For the next year or so, I divided my time between Tennessee and California. I was working in Los Angeles and living in an apartment, but my office was still in Nashville. My furniture and belongings were in storage in Tennessee. I made the decision to bring them to California, as it was becoming more of my permanent home. My parents helped pack the truck of my belongings and offered to make the drive across country in lieu of hiring a moving company. I accepted their generous offer. They set out in the truck, and I flew back to California to await their arrival in three days or so.

We spoke several times while they were en route; all was well. A couple of moving guys and my friend Amy were there when my parents arrived. At the loading dock behind my apartment building, we all stood expectantly as the door was rolled up. Instantly, we knew something had gone terribly wrong. Inside the truck, the contents, which had barely fit when we packed them in Nashville, had been reduced to a jumbled pile half the size. I could see the arm of an antique rocking chair all splintered and sticking up like some horribly broken bone. A marble tabletop was in three or four chunks. Glass was everywhere. Nothing we unloaded was in one piece.

I turned away to cry. The loss felt so personal and deep, as though everything I loved was destroyed, broken, or marred. My parents felt terrible and had no idea what could have happened. The two guys who came to help with the move just shook their heads in disbelief. We all felt like the truck's contents looked: crushed.

With not much I could unload, I decided to put everything in storage until I could sort through it all. The next day we all met at a storage unit to see what might be left worth saving. We had to carry many things to the dumpster in pieces. So much had been lost. Finally down to the bottom, I saw a broken frame, and in the rubble on the truck floor, I saw little pieces of colored glass that I recognized from a stained-glass window. This special piece was an antique from an old house and was a gift to me from my friend Audrey. She and her husband, Randy, had bought three pieces of this stained glass at an auction, a transom and two windows. They planned to use them in a house they hoped to build some-day. Audrey had given me one of these windows for a Christmas present. It was just too much.

We would come to find out later that the air-ride suspension on the truck had not been connected, so while it seemed smooth sailing in the front of the truck, everything in the back had been bouncing around as if on a trampoline—for two thousand miles.

The loss seemed so very personal in light of the other events of my life. To many people looking at the outside, and understandably so, my life and marriage had seemed smooth sailing. Unfortunately, that wasn't the reality on the inside. It all had tumbled out of the "truck" of our relationship and lay in pieces on the ground.

Now divorced and looking at all of the stained glass, it was a heartbreaking picture. Just rubble. I wept with a sadness of the ages, for all that had been so horribly broken—my parents' mar-riage, my self-esteem as a little girl, and now my own marriage. Yet, even as I sobbed for what was lost, I knew in my soul that God was holding me and healing me. I'd grown deeper and clearer about what real life could look like for me, and while this vision had come at exorbitant cost, it would not be wasted.

I could never have known at the time that this philosophy of fresh-brewed life, which had been formed looking backward at the fragments of my shattered childhood and in the shadow of the difficulties of my marriage, would ultimately be the hope of my future. I didn't know it would become my life's message. I couldn't imagine that God would allow me to see something more in the broken pieces of other people's lives in addition to my own. All I could see at the time were broken, ground-up, fragmented dreams—but because of fresh-brewed life, I did have hope.

My parents, Amy, and I unloaded the last bits of furniture, threw away the last pieces and other bits that could not be salvaged, and swept the truck floor clean. We pulled the door down, and I prayed that God had closed the chapter on all the breaking, and the healing would begin.

And slowly, but surely, it did. God, in his infinite mercy, gave me what I needed most and wanted least: community. I felt adrift on my own iceberg, mostly out of fear that the truth would not set me free but rather imprison me for speaking it. Cold and alone, I washed up on the "Island of Misfit Toys," known to many as Women of Faith. A band of sister pilgrims, they made a place for me at the table of grace and bid me stay. And the most amazing thing happened. Women came out of the shadows to share their stories of pain and how they found real life in the midst of their brokenness. Women of Faith became a safe harbor and a launching point for me to write again.

On my second Christmas in California, I opened a present from my friend Amy. The box was big, and I was unwrapping carefully and very curiously, until what I saw made my breathing stop. There were fragments of stained glass, and for a moment I thought . . . but I caught myself and just kept unwrapping. It couldn't be. My mind was in overdrive. *Were these the pieces I last saw in the bottom of the truck at the storage room?* I looked at Amy, and she nodded. I started to cry like a baby. I looked at the glass and then back to Amy, then at the glass. *Oh, dear God—look at what she's done with these pieces!*

Back on that awful day at the storage unit, Amy kept the trash bag from the last load. She confessed she couldn't bear to throw it all away, so she'd kept the whole thing—not even knowing at the time what she would do with it. The big, green bag held pieces of glass, dust, and everything we'd swept from the bottom of the truck. She sifted through all the junk to find every piece of stained glass. She then researched until she found an artisan who saw the value in the old glass pieces and was thrilled with the chance to make something new from them.

I couldn't take my eyes off the stained-glass piece in front of me. The original pieces had been put together in a remarkable new way. It was beautiful if you didn't know the story of how it came to be. But knowing what I knew about those pieces—knowing they'd been on the floor of the truck, with shards of other glass, dirt, and wood, and that I'd thrown them away—made the new piece one of the most exquisite gifts I've ever received.

Today, it hangs in my home in a window where the light shines through it, showing off its glorious colors and unique shapes. People comment on it, not knowing the story, and if time permits, I never miss a chance to tell a little about the window, if only to watch the appreciation of its simple beauty deepen. It is the very picture of my fresh-brewed life.

So now, almost eight years later, I'm holding my cup in the circle of women who have invited me to be their weekend guest. The women I came to serve were serving me. Everything from them had gone into that cup: the pain, the joy, the stories, the suffering, the experiences they were afraid they couldn't survive. I thought of the prayer of Jesus in his deepest hour of anguish.

"If possible, God, please let this cup pass from me." Before that moment, I'd never thought about the cup Jesus mentioned. It was the cup that held the suffering of the world—all the pain, all the sin, all the anguish. No one wants the brokenness. No one wants what that cup holds. I didn't, the women sitting around me didn't, and even the Son of God didn't. But the cup didn't pass, and Jesus drank it to the bottom, that we might have life—and a fresh-brewed one at that.

More than a decade after penning the first words that started this book, I want to make the same assurance to you but with a confidence that only suffering and time can bring. If you will offer the whole-bean essence of who you are (even if you aren't fully sure yet), surrender to the inevitable roasting and grinding of this world, and trust that the love of God will pour over all the broken pieces (fragments, shards, and hunks), your very life will be transformed into something more beautiful and remarkable than you could have ever imagined.

Just about the time you feel deep satisfaction for the healing and peace that God has brought, you will feel a tap on your shoulder and see a woman standing in front of you, holding an empty cup. For the first time, you'll know exactly what to do. You will pour from your life, trying humbly to explain what defies explanation: the miracle of what you are pouring out. You'll look up only to see another woman and another cup, and for a moment you may fear you won't have enough. Then you'll realize that God has taken the life you've offered, the self you've surrendered, and by his great love has multiplied everything, so you can pour away. After all, you didn't make this fresh brew; God did, by pouring his love over the broken pieces you thought you should throw away.

So pour it out—and fill 'er up.

Bibliography

Ban Breathnach, Sarah. *Simple Abundance: A Daybook of Comfort and Joy*. New York: Warner Books, 1995.

Buford, Bob. *Half Time*. Grand Rapids, MI: Zondervan, 1994.

Darabont, Frank. *The Shawshank Redemption* (screenplay). Produced by Niki Marvin. 1994.

Dillard, Annie. *Teaching a Stone to Talk*. New York: Harper Perennial, 1982.

Douglas, Susan J. *Where the Girls Are: Growing Up Female with the Mass Media*. New York: Random House, 1995.

Griffin, Emilie. *Clinging: The Experience of Prayer*. New York: McCracken Press, 1994.

Groom, Nancy. *Heart to Heart About Men*. Colorado Springs: NavPress, 1995.

Lambert, Ellen Zetzel. *The Face of Love*. Boston: Beacon Press, 1995.

Lee-Thorp, Karen and Cynthia Hicks. *Why Beauty Matters*. Colorado Springs: NavPress, 1997.

L'Engle, Madeline. *Walking on Water*. Wheaton, IL: Harold Shaw Publishers, 1972.

Lerner, Harriet Goldhor. *The Dance of Anger*. New York: Harper and Row, 1985.

Nouwen, Henri. *Life of the Beloved: Spiritual Living in a Secular World.* New York: Crossroad, 1992.

_____. *Here and Now: Living in the Spirit.* New York: Crossroad, 1994.

O'Connor, Elizabeth. *Letters to Scattered Pilgrims.* New York: Harper and Row, 1979.

SARK. *Succulent Wild Woman.* New York: Simon and Schuster, 1997.

Smalley, Gary. Marriage and Relations - Video Answer by Gary Smalley. National Institute of Marriage website, http://iquestions.com/video/view/129.

Wells, Ann. "A Story to Live By," *Los Angeles Times,* 1997.

Discussion Questions

Chapter 1: Surrender to God

1. When have you ever felt a need to pretend or hide? Can you identify when this may have first started? Why do people continue in the pattern of pretending?
2. What is the difference between doing things for God and being with God? Is the distinction important?
3. The author wrote, "What you do doesn't determine who you are in the core of your being, but it does reflect what you believe (right or wrongly) is at the core of your being." Think about this concept and name a few of the things this reveals you believe at your core.
4. What might we have trouble being honest with God about? What, if anything, does this reveal about us in other relationships?
5. When have you ever seen God in "disguise"? Describe your moment of recognition that came in the moment or later.
6. For it to be well with our souls, why ought we not to skip around in this hymn? What difference would it make if our sin were nailed to the cross "in part"?

7. What is the great challenge in surrendering? Why does or doesn't it come naturally to us? How could our personality affect our ability to surrender? What about our perspective on what we are surrendering to?

Chapter 2: Encounter Your Journal

1. Have you ever written a poem? What was the circumstance that prompted you to write something? Why do people journal or not?

2. What are some of the ways you would benefit by bringing your heart to paper? What are some of the reasons you're resistant?

3. Why should a journal be off-limits to others? Have you respected or violated that in the past?

4. Do you find it easier to *do* or to *be*? Are you more prone to tell yourself why you can't do something or to try to find ways you can?

5. How can a journal serve as a "therapist's couch"? How about as a spiritual tool?

6. What are some of the ways your day might change if you recorded some of your observations or things you were grateful for? What about ways it might improve your parenting or your marriage?

7. Name a few ways that just being aware of our choices can change our perspective?

8. Creativity can be strengthened by journaling. Specifically, how can you increase your creativity by using a journal?

Chapter 3: Listen to Your Longings

1. What longings do you have in your life? What are the big

things that are genuine disappointments? How have you re-acted to them?

2. If you are honest, has the net effect of the disappointments driven you away from God—or brought you closer?

3. What happens to us when we fall for the false response to longings and become "spectators"? Will this free us from pain in our lives?

4. What happens when we become hypercritical "evaluators"? Will this way of approaching disappointment lead us to more joy?

5. Do you agree with the distinction between wishes, dreams, and longings? Do these categories accurately reflect what you know of yourself and others?

6. What does it mean to respond positively to the "holes" that are supposed to be there?

7. How can we avoid "medicating" our longings and use them instead as "treasure maps" to help us discover what God has in store for us?

Chapter 4: Embrace Your Beauty

1. What would it take for us to trust that the Lord has gently created each of us to be beautiful in our own way?

2. Where do most women you know get their images of beauty? How have those images been formed in the past? How are they still being formed today?

3. Think about occasions in your own life when you were at odds with the world's ideals of beauty. What false responses should we avoid?

4. Do you agree that women are torn over how we see ourselves? If so, what does that do to us inside?

5. What negative voices do you hear in your life about how you look (e.g., from your past, your family, our culture)? What happens to us when we listen to such voices rather than to God?

6. What could it look like in practice to be comfortable with who God made us to be? To be God's "beloved"? To embrace our beauty?

7. In what ways might our lives change if we pressed deeper into such truths?

8. How do we discover the secret of being an alive, passionate woman in this world?

9. Are there women in your life—a daughter, a sister, a friend, a colleague—who need encouragement to discover the beauty God has given them? How will you share with them what you have learned here about real beauty?

Chapter 5: Interview Your Anger

1. Do you agree that women today are not allowed to be angry? Do you sense a double standard? If so, where do you see evidence of this? How does it make you feel?

2. Why do you think we may be afraid of being perceived as angry?

3. What would it mean if you were angry?

4. In what ways do people often try to deny their anger but only end up expressing it in different forms, such as a critical spirit?

5. Are there places in your life where you are mad at God? How are you handling them?

6. Psychologists tell us that anger is made up of fear, frustrations, and hurt. What might you be fearful of? Where have your feelings been hurt? Why are you frustrated?

7. Have you slowed down enough to interview yourself and take stock of yourself emotionally? Have you shared the results with a close friend?

8. What are the benefits of journaling that make it a key tool in the interviewing process? What role, if any, does it play in your life?

9. What are the main "fuel dumps" in your life?

10. Where are you in danger of infuriating yourself by compromising yourself?

11. Is there a relationship in your life that was broken long ago that has you "limping" today? What can you do to "set it" right?

Chapter 6: Savor Your Sexuality

1. On a scale of 1 to 10, how satisfied are you with your sexual relationship with your husband? Why is it (or is it not) an accurate expression of who you are? On that same scale, how well do you feel "known"? In what way do you see the two questions as related?

2. Why do you think men take sexual postponement (not necessarily rejection) so personally? In what areas can we relate to this personal rejection as women?

3. Have you ever been tempted to "go away" during sex? Why do you think this occurred or still occurs? Are there strategies that you can consider after reading this chapter that might help combat this?

4. How honestly have you dealt with any sexual pain from your past? What are some of the difficulties past sexual experiences can bring into a current relationship? How can we know if we are free from the past?

5. How connected do you feel to your senses? What sense are you most connected to and why that particular one? Are there ways you can think of to awaken your heart and soul to a few others? List them here.

6. What are your least favorite things about your body? How does your opinion of these areas shape your sexual expression—publicly and privately? Are there any of these dislikes that could be easily changed?

7. What are the areas of your life that you feel the best about? In other words, not thinking just of your body, what things would you say you do well? How does your opinion of these areas shape your sexual expression—publicly and privately?

8. How can you break a cycle of shame and rejection over sex if you're stuck? What can embracing the *imago dei* in your soul and in your marriage do to help?

Chapter 7: Celebrate Your Friendships

1. Why might we find it hard to celebrate in general? Did you grow up feeling celebrated in your family? Why would that even make a difference?

2. What would you say is your greatest need in friendship? To have fewer, closer friends or more friends or just a couple of good friends? Who are some of your friendship models?

3. How did you feel about friendship growing up? Was it easy for you to make and keep friends?

4. In what way are friendships with adult women harder or easier than the friendships we had as girls?

5. If you identified in your journaling that you are too busy for friendships, what factors have contributed to this conclusion? What are ways to begin to change them?

6. What does it look like to push our husbands or boyfriends into a role that a good girlfriend should play? What are the warning signs we could heed before we do it again?

7. Why is a friendship with God so easy to take for granted? What is the cost of doing so?

8. In the chapter, Audrey's friend made a choice not to have flowers because flowers attract bees. What choices have you made out of fear that cause you to miss something beautiful?

Chapter 8: Change Your World

1. Think over your life. In all your busyness, how can you make sure you have your priorities in place—things to which you are purposefully, passionately committed? If you don't know what those things are, how can you begin to find them?

2. How do you pursue your "passion," what the author calls "the one thing" without becoming selfish?

3. Is it only a "man's thing" to pursue purpose and significance in life? What does our culture say? What does God say?

4. How do you and your friends measure up to the author's observation about women who complete all the tasks but have no joy in the process?

5. If you could have any life in the world, whose would it be and why? What is God calling you to do?

6. What are some of the ways that women postpone their lives and put them on hold by avoiding their passion?

7. What do you think it means when we talk about changing the world we live in? Is this happening in your life? What are some of the ways you know that you are changing the world?

8. Discuss how you and perhaps a few of your close friends may pursue this goal more consistently.

9. Try a "Receiving Praise Day." When someone gives you a compliment, just receive it. No ifs, ands, or buts—just a simple thank you, period.

Chapter 9: Enrich Your Relationships

1. What seems most important and relevant to your life in the author's distinction between knowing and doing? What relationship could benefit the most if you could move from knowing to doing? Could too much "knowledge" be hurting us in specific ways you can think of personally?

2. Why can't marriage eliminate loneliness?

3. In what areas are you tempted to "stuff" the holes to medicate the pain of empty places? Can you identify where those holes may have come from? What are some strategies to employ that will allow them to heal?

4. In what ways do we look to others to determine our worth? While we may know they can't, and they may know as well, what can keep us from doing this going forward?

5. Can you think of a time early in your life that your trust in someone was betrayed or broken? How do you think this shaped your life and/or your ability to trust?

6. What are some of the qualities generally found in a trustworthy person? What is the best way to determine if someone is worthy of trust?

7. Which relationships can you think of that need to be fortified or enriched by trust? How can you add this important ingredient?

Chapter 10: Enjoy Your Freedom

1. What evidence would support whether your heart is growing or shrinking as you've gotten older?

2. Why would it be considered freedom to take someone at his or her word? Why do you find it easy or difficult to take what people say at face value?

3. Would freedom in your life look like taking more time for yourself or making more time for other activities that don't focus on yourself? Why can each be considered freedom?

4. What kind of freedom is there in resisting the urge to control how you appear to others? Why does it take more energy to manage what other people think?

5. Describe a time in your life when you felt you may have needed the "walls."

6. In the directed journaling, you were instructed to write about three prisons of your own making. Pick one prison that has had an especially powerful hold over you and write down some of the whispers you've heard inside that cell. Have you ever retreated to prison for safety?

7. Take one area of your life (could be financial, professional, relational, even physical) where you hunger for more freedom. Look at each of the components carefully, and think through the price, form your plan, and pray for the power to move toward freedom in this one area.

8. What would a few items on "A Day in the Life of Your Freedom" look like? How could your choosing to be free in this way affect the lives of those around you, positively or negatively?

Acknowledgments

The original version of *Fresh-Brewed Life* would have been an unopened, vacuum-sealed bag of beans on a shelf somewhere were it not for the urging and contributions of a few very special people. I'd like to say thanks to:

Robert Wolgemuth, my literary agent and friend, for the encouragement to use my voice.

My celebrating friends: Audrey, Angela, and Denise, who sculpted me into a friend.

John, Betty, Ken, and Esther, thank you for drinking cups of fresh-brewed life and helping me remove the bitter to make it better.

My trusted associate and friend, Mary Bowman. Thank you for walking alongside me and sharing this journey with me.

My mother, for loving me deeply enough to encourage me to write our story, but also for living in the kind of freedom that would allow me to share it.

Mike Hyatt at Thomas Nelson, for believing in my voice, and

Brian Hampton, Judith Pierson, and the rest of the fresh-brewed Thomas Nelson team, who thought we should put on another pot and offer more cups to the world.

My courageous companions at Women of Faith, you became the hands of God as you picked up my broken pieces and refused to throw them away. M and Lulu, with eyes to see the artwork of the divine, you saw some strange value in this weeping woman, and I will be forever grateful.

Amy, for giving me a picture of redemption worth far more than a thousand words—more like the fifty-five thousand on these pages.

My cleat-wearing, snorkel-toting, spaghetti-making, support-giving tribe in Santa Monica. You're robust, flavorful, and good to the last drop. Oh my, how I love you.

About the Author

Nicole Johnson is a writer and performer of original drama, with more than twenty-five years' experience. As an actor, producer, and author, her unique gift sets her apart in the world of communication. Through her work with Women of Faith and other organizations, Nicole's work has touched the lives and hearts of millions. She resides in Santa Monica, California, with her husband and two children.

CPSIA information can be obtained
at www.ICGtesting.com
Printed in the USA
LVHW040045230219
608526LV00007B/91

9 781400 203154